In Chains for My Country
Crusading for the British Southern Cameroons

Nfor N. Nfor

Langaa Research & Publishing CIG
Mankon, Bamenda

Publisher:
Langaa RPCIG
Langaa Research & Publishing Common Initiative Group
P.O. Box 902 Mankon
Bamenda
North West Region
Cameroon
Langaagrp@gmail.com
www.langaa-rpcig.net

Distributed in and outside N. America by African Books Collective
orders@africanbookscollective.com
www.africanbookcollective.com

ISBN: 9956-792-04-7

© Nfor, N. Nfor 2014

DISCLAIMER
All views expressed in this publication are those of the author and do not necessarily reflect the views of Langaa RPCIG.

Dedication

Dedicated to Amidu Bel SUIKA, Boniface LAIGHA, Terence SELA, struck down by the mortal bullets of the occupation forces of La Republique du Cameroun on October 1, 2001 in Kumbo, Bui County, and many other Southern Cameroonians slain by the annexationist regime.

And to Pa Stephen NDI, who, on retirement from the British colonial army and on return from WW11 has since 1947, dedicated his entire life to the legitimate struggle for the independence of British Southern Cameroons and dignity of his people: and to all defenders of human FREEDOM, JUSTICE and EQUALITY.

To all who have died, in the cause of the nonviolent struggle led by the SCNC for the Restoration of the STATEHOOD and INDEPENDENCE of British Southern Cameroons, your blood watered the tree of LIBERTY. You will forever be remembered for paying the supreme price.

Table of Contents

Acknowledgement... vii
Preface.. xi
Abbreviations and Acronyms........................... xvii

1. Introduction.. 1
2. Difficult To Believe..................................... 11
3. The Real World of Bamenda Central Prison....... 21
4. Within the Iron Fence................................. 29
5. The Bitter-Sweet... 39
6. Through the Eye of Prison Detention............. 45
7. Not the First of Its Kind............................. 55
8. A Taste of Hell by Extension...................... 79
9. The Root of the Reign of Evil.................... 91
10. It Knows No Limits.................................. 107
11. Fifty-Six Theses Justifying the restoration of the Statehood of British Southern Cameroons... 125
12. Poems.. 145
13. Conclusion... 151

Bibliography... 161

Acknowledgement

Man, by nature, is a gregarious being. Even love and hatred, unity and disunity, co-operation and non-co-operation, agreement and disagreement, justice and injustice, among others, are recurrent decimals of any given human society because of the nature of the human mind and the fact that man lives in society. And living in society there is the constant struggle for self and collective identity. There is therefore nothing achieved in human society that was conceived in isolation, planned in isolation and executed to a finish without the influence and input of another man. This has its genesis, I think, in the creation of man. In the book of Genesis 1:26 we hear God talk of "Let us make man in our image…"

Even if a thing could be conceived and executed to a finish by one mind, it cannot be work of this dimension and nature.

What we must know is that man, though an animal is higher than all other animals, thanks to his spiritual and creative power of reason. Man though born without weapons to defend himself against other more powerful animals, the mind is man's greatest weapon and tool for self-defence and achievement for a meaningful and better life.

Man excels to great heights through effective exploitation of his mind. He descends to the abyss when under domination his right to freedom of thought, opinion, speech and assembly is denied through the brutal use of instruments of repression. Man's rich potentials blossom when he is enjoying his full rights and freedom. And as a gregarious being he freely interacts with his fellow humans and in the beauty of God's nature enjoys the constant exchange of ideas with his fellow man.

It will be a mark of ingratitude, if I do not thank the agents of the annexationist Yaoundé regime that arrested, tortured and mercilessly detained us under life-threatening circumstances. With all due respect, "In Chains for My Country" is consequent upon their inhumanity and zeal to re-enact and sustain what civilised man has condemned and banned, namely, "annexation, colonialism, foreign domination, alien rule, and torture. It is in condemning and working resolutely to achieve human freedom, equality, dignity, and justice that human progress is attained. The coloniser is always in the minority, against truth, justice, legality and greater humanity. Standing on the wrong side of history, he fails because he is against human progress and dignity. He is always wrong.

Sincere special thanks go to our Lawyers – Justice A. N. Njamnsi (rtd), Justice Nyo Wakai (rtd), Barristers Pius Njobara, Harmony Bobga and others who challenged our detention in the Bamenda High Court as illegal and worked hard to have us released. But the harder they worked, the more the proconsuls and occupation forces devised strategies to keep us behind the bars longer, part of which was blaming the lawyers for making a mountain out of a molehill, thus making it difficult for the administration to show its magnanimity in releasing us. An expansionist state with its occupation forces that suck the blood of the enslaved being magnanimous!! This sounds like the lion priding itself of being fair to the lamb it devoirs for breakfast.

My gratitude also goes to the Southern Cameroonian patriots of Bamenda and beyond who sustained and prayed for us without which we could have all perished in detention.

As difficult as it is to enumerate such a multitude, it will suffice, on behalf of the many, to name these few – Mrs Regina Mankefor, Cecilia Ngwatum, Mary Tawah, who mobilised the Takembeng mothers to feed their children fighting for justice, the wives of the detainees, family members and friends, the many SCNC activists who toiled day and night for our welfare, the many who prayed day and night for God to do to us what He did to Paul and Silas while in prison for preaching the truth.

Unreserved thanks are here for Martin A. Ngock, Zachs Ndeh, Fidelis Chinkwo, my junior brother Dr Napoleon K. Nfor, Caleb Yerima, Julius Nyugap Ndi, among others, who like "the remains of corn flour that need not fear boiling water on the fire" as the Limbum proverb goes, went the extra mile in doing what needed be done.

My prison detention inmates, especially I.M. Sona, Pa Stephen Ndi who showed keen interest in what I was doing, read some of the scattered scripts and made valuable contribution cannot be forgotten. They were a regular storehouse of renewed strength, encouragement, sound ideas and refreshment. This is sincerely highly appreciated.

Finally, my thanks go to my wife, Mrs Mary Nan Nfor and children, my mother Ma Winto Mbebu whose sweet memories of the Endeley and Foncha Governments in Buea see the devil in everything that happens today. I owe a debt of gratitude to Mrs Josephine Fru Tumabang, who under stress of our detention patiently put my scattered writings in readable manuscript. Without the moral support of these *"In Chains for My Country: Crusading for the British Southern Cameroons"* would not have seen the light of day.

NFOR N. NFOR
Bamenda,

Preface

"*In Chains for My Country: Crusading for the British Southern Cameroons*", is an account of prison detention experiences following the arbitrary arrest and detention of SCNC leaders and some activists in 2001. Though the recapitulation here is as I saw and experienced it, "*In Chains for My Country: Crusading for the British Southern Cameroons*" is the saga of a people suffocating under black neo-colonial rule which I have christened neo-apartheid.

The failure of the decolonisation process in 1961 coupled with the self-seeking treacherous behaviour of some of the Southern Cameroons leaders who could not grapple with the implication of "independence by joining" opened a sad page in the history of human kind. This sad page of the history of double standards in the process of decolonisation underlies the state of affairs as portrayed in this book. Every cause has an effect!

While studies portray the then leaders as reluctant converts to "independence by joining" they could not summon courage and learning from history unite and mobilise their people to reject the plebiscite like Ahmed Sekou Toure of Guinea, Conakry, who in 1958 mobilised his people and they voted against the French Community, an imposition from France aimed at denying the people sovereign independence and perpetrating French imperial rule. Yet Guinea (Conakry) was a French colony. This is the most lamentable thing which Southern Cameroonians, including the then leaders, who have lived under la République du Cameroun's reign of terror find it hard to forgive. The reality on the ground, a credit to the British

Southern Cameroonian people, is that neither the UN nor the UK had any right whatsoever to impose the manner in which British Southern Cameroons had to gain independence. The choice, as upheld by the UN Charter and international instruments, was/is theirs to make and once made to be respected by all.

The question that remains to be answered is why the UK, the Administering Authority did, introduce and imposed the criteria of size and economic viability and denied the right to national sovereign existence for British Southern Cameroons?

Secondly, why did the democratic nations of the UN accept this condition when neither Art. 76 (b) of the UN Charter, the Trusteeship Agreement, (remember the *sacred trust*), nor UNGA Resolution 1514 of 1960 prescribe any conditions for attainment of independence?

It should be appreciated that colonialism, in whatever manner it manifests itself, like slavery and slave trade, has been declared a crime against humanity and banned in the interest of world peace, democracy and human progress. To push these universal values to the fore, independence for all dependent territories was unconditionally made a right of the people concerned and not a privilege. The Administering Authority, as made abundantly clear in the Trusteeship Agreement, the UN Charter and UNGA Resolution 1514 of 1960, had no right whatsoever to prescribe preconditions and impose hurdles for the Trust territory.

Thirdly, why did the UN fail to implement UNGA Resolution 1608 of April 21, 1961?

Fourthly, did la République du Cameroun's vote against forming a federal union of two states "EQUAL IN STATUS" with British Southern Cameroons (UNGA Resolution 1608) not negate the UN's experiment in forming a federal union between two incompatible nations and peoples?

Fifthly, since UNGA Resolution 1608 was predicated on the plebiscite result, did the failure of the UN to implement the Resolution not declare the outcome of the plebiscite null and void and of no effect?

Sixthly, considering the fact that British Southern Cameroons was a UN Trust and the UK only administered the territory "a Sacred Trust" on behalf of the UN and in view of the fact that decolonisation was/is indisputably a UN responsibility, by what instrument did la République du Cameroun impose its jurisdiction over British Southern Cameroons on 1st October 1961 and has continued to do same in spite of legitimate protests by Southern Cameroonians? Why have the UN and all democratic nations of the world, including those that voted for British Southern Cameroons independence in the 4th Committee of the UNGA, continued to keep sealed lips in the face of gross violation of the rights of the people of British Southern Cameroons?

"*In Chains for My Country: Crusading for the British Southern Cameroons*" is only one more sincere effort, like others before, such as "Prisoner Without A Crime" by Albert W. Mukong, "Inside The Fence" by Nyo Wakai, among others, to bring to the kind and urgent attention of the world community the most unbearable plight of a people in this third millennium. Without doubt this should stare world conscience for positive action. The urgency of the matter demands that the UNSG or a democratic nation under preventive diplomacy should put the British Southern Cameroons Question on the agenda of the UN for constructive debate and adoption of a comprehensive plan of action for effective decolonisation.

Arch Bishop Desmond Tutu, the great South African crusader against apartheid warns and admonishes human kind against trying to sit on the fence; *"If you are neutral in situations of injustice, you have chosen the side of the oppressor. If an elephant has its foot on the tail of a mouse and you say you are neutral, the mouse will not appreciate your neutrality."* Indeed to say the least, this is no neutrality. It is collaboration with the oppressor and conspiracy against the oppressed.

This explains why Martin Luther King declares, "History will have to record that the greatest tragedy of this period of social transition was not the strident clamour of bad people but the appalling silence of the good people." And he concludes, "In the end we will remember not the words our enemies but the silence of our friends."

British Southern Cameroons problem has its genesis within the UN system. The UN as a matter of urgency should accomplish its unfinished mission in British Southern Cameroons.

Such timely positive action is the only road map to avert Rwandan type genocide for no people can in perpetuity surrender to the unbearable claws of foreign domination, alien rule, assimilation, dehumanisation and the naked plunder of their natural resources. The botched decolonisation process makes British Southern Cameroons a painful scar on the conscience of the UN system and the international community in general.

The only regret I have is my inability to have had *"In Chains for My Country: Crusading for the British Southern Cameroons"* published immediately. The delay has not in any manner or way defaced the message as it was conceived and written in prison. But the inevitable delay has deprived some outstanding colleagues and compatriots, namely, "Prison

Graduates who had the baptism of fire," as we call it, whose contribution and support I very much cherish, of seeing and appreciating the final clean copy. Close associates such as Pa Stephen Ndi, Mrs. Regina Mankefor, Dr M. N. Luma, Justice A. N. Njamnsi (rtd) among others who made their enviable mark and have been called to eternal rest will forever be remembered. *"In Chains for My Country: Crusading for the British Southern Cameroons"* is indeed a monument in their name and will forever stand and be cherished as their testament to the struggle for the restoration of the sovereign statehood of British Southern Cameroons.

The real irredeemable regret is however that some manuscript and my prison dairy were lost as we were unceremoniously made to leave the night we were forced out as narrated in the book. Many more vital documents, records of the defunct Government of British Southern Cameroons have been lost or destroyed by agents of the annexationist Yaoundé regime to distort and annihilate the history and distinct identity of British Southern Cameroons. Comparatively, therefore, while I lament what I lost that fateful night is not up to one millionth of what British Southern Cameroons lost when under military escorts, lorry loads of vital government documents and records were ferried from Buea to Yaoundé in 1972. That act alone was vandalistic for these important documents can never be recovered. And what is more, the then actors with inside knowledge have all joined their ancestors in the great beyond.

Nfor N. Nfor

Cross section of Delegates at Mount Mary Maternity Hall, Nfor N. Nfor in suit in between Pa S. Ndi & lady, Buea, 1993

Abbreviations & Acronyms

AAC- All Anglophone Conference
ACHPR – African Commission on Human and Peoples' Rights
ANC – African National Congress
Les Anglos or Anglofools – Derogatory name used for Southern Cameroonians
AT – Awaiting Trial
AU – African Union
BMM – Brigades Mixtes Mobiles
BTTC- Baptist Teachers Training College
CAM – Cameroon Anglophone Movement
CAT – (Southern) Cameroons Air Transport
CDC – Cameroon Development Corporation
CEO – Chief Executive Officer
CNU – Cameroon National Union
CPDM – Cameroon People's Democratic Movement
GCE – General Certificate of Education
GDP – Gross Domestic Product
GMI – Mobile Intervention Unit
HRDG – Human Rights Defense Group
ICCPR - International Covenant on Civil and Political Rights
KNDP – Kamerun National Democratic Party
LN – League of Nations
MINAT – Ministère d'Administration Territorial
MP – Member of Parliament
NSC – National Sovereign Conference
NPMB – National Produce Marketing Board
OAU – Organisation of African Unity
SCARM – Southern Cameroons Restoration Movement

SCNC – Southern Cameroons National Council
SDF – Social Democratic Front
SDECE – Service de Documentation Extérieure et de Contre-Espionnage
SEDOC – Service de Documentation
SNH – Société Nationale Hydrocarboné
SONARA – Société Nationale de Raffinage
UC – Union Camerounaise
UDHR- Universal Declaration of Human Rights
UDI – Unilateral Declaration of Independence
UK – United Kingdom of Great Britain and Northern Ireland
UNGA – United Nations General Assembly
UNO – United Nations Organisation
UNSG – United Nations Secretary General
UPC – Union des Populations du Cameroun
VOA – Voice of America
WCC – World Council of Churches

1

Introduction

On October 1, 2001 British Southern Cameroonians in their numbers came out all over the national territory, to commemorate the 40th Anniversary of the confiscation of their Independence by la République du Cameroun. This was in response to the call by the Southern Cameroons National Council (SCNC).

When posters were produced and invitations sent out to the UN Secretary General and all UN Member nations that voted for the independence of British Southern Cameroons, the Yaoundé regime of President Paul Biya put troops on red alert. In addition to the trigger-happy occupation forces spread all over the Southern Cameroons, heavy reinforcements were ordered into the territory. The francophone proconsuls and their agents and lackeys living on conscience money embarked on smear campaign promising hell and elimination to any "subversive elements", that is, patriotic Southern Cameroonians and freedom fighters. Some who pass around as the "true leaders" campaigning for the international personality of the Southern Cameroons even issued circulars warning Southern Cameroonians not to heed the call of SCNC leaders and come out for the commemoration. They even blackmailed SCNC Leaders as sponsored agents of la République du Cameroun. Sponsored agents of la République du Cameroun challenging the status quo and taking the risk to publicly commemorate Southern Cameroons confiscated independence!

But the impact of the commemoration brought the Southern Cameroons legitimate struggle against annexation and colonial occupation to limelight. It was a turning point in the nature of the nonviolent struggle with the people determined to take their destiny in their hands. These agents of distraction were quick to back paddle when they saw that the population was with the SCNC. As we the leaders were behind bars, retired Ambassador Henry Fossung was quick to claim credit and announce that he organised the celebrations and those killed were his supporters. He shamelessly tried to use the killings, our detention and torture to his credit for self-aggrandisement.

For the proconsuls and the occupation forces to prove that they meant business, arrests started one week to October 1. Prince Humphrey Mbinglo, Chairman of the Northern Zone, was the first victim. His vice Mr Henry Nyah soon followed. Publicity materials destined for various SCNC structures were seized at car parks as spies, made up of Southern Cameroons Judases and imported francophones were planted twenty-four hours round the clock to monitor the movement of SCNC leaders and suspects.

On Monday 25th September gendarmes and police who came in three vehicles, two of which came from outside the province, raided Pa Stephen Ndi's house at Cow Street, Bamenda. Pa Ndi, an octogenarian, was arbitrarily arrested, tortured, detained and subjected to several hours of interrogation despite his evident poor health. The three vehicles on departure from Pa Ndi's residence were filled with old CAM/SCARM materials, SCNC documents, membership cards, publicity materials, high quality national flags of the Federal Republic of Southern Cameroons and even some money that was in Pa Stephen Ndi's keeping. Till today nothing has been recovered.

One other spectacular arrest was that of Tata Francis who printed the Southern Cameroons T-shirts. He was arrested with his four-year old son, Noel Wam Tata, who clung to his neck as he (Tata Francis) was tortured and carried and thrown into the back of an open truck at night. This baby was detained for four days by the gendarmes. With the father (Francis Tata) on his back on the bare cement floor, the boy lived the experience of hell on earth in the gendarme cell on his father's chest.

To avoid further arrests which the occupation forces saw as the only means by which the planned celebration could be punctured and nipped in the bud, the leaders decided to lie low in order to shoot high on October 1. Their houses, which were twenty-four hours under plain-clothes police surveillance, were abandoned. This we successfully did. This greatly encouraged the population many of whom were on their knees praying. The Lord heard their prayers and answered, as was the case with the Israelites of old (Exodus 3:7-9).

On October 1, the tensed political climate notwithstanding, the population happily applauded their leaders as they emerged to address them and lead in the Anniversary Match on the Bamenda Commercial Avenue.

In Bamenda, the main centre of the commemoration, the occupation forces armed to the teeth had taken positions at all known strategic points under the cover of night before dawn. On the acclaim of the leaders on the Bamenda Commercial Avenue, furious looking troops descended on the leaders like hawks and vultures descend on a dead cow. In keeping with our Motto: "The Force of Argument, Not the Argument of Force", we offered no resistance for we were prepared, once the point was made.

Arrests and brutalisation equally took place in other major towns such as Nkambe, Ndu, Kumba, Mutengene, Mamfe, Buea, among others. In Kumbo, Bui County, gendarmes opened fire on peaceful celebrants and three were murdered instantly while many were wounded. One of the wounded died some months later. Was this the price Bui paid for having two of its sons, Mr Christopher Nsahlai and Colonel Yenwo, few months back, appointed Minister and Army General, respectively, of la République du Cameroun? Being appointed a minister or army general under an imperial regime is of no consequence to the millions subjected to brutish rule. Such a person simply bags the title of traitor of his kith and kin.

While in Prison these tribulations and the reality of the degradation of our people tormented my conscience and soul persistently. The question that kept coming is, "Is the Southern Cameroons nation a historical, cultural and legal reality"?

In my humble and sincere effort to give my fellow compatriots the necessary political education, I am inspired by Osagyefor Kwame Nkrumah of Ghana who, while campaigning from prison used toilet tissue as writing material. Convinced about the legality and legitimacy of his campaign for the freedom of his people he was not deterred by his confinement behind the cold solitary walls of a colonial prison. His message and determination inspired the masses and they rose in unison and defended their right to independence. The Gold Coast became independent Ghana, the first colony south of the Sahara to become independent in 1957.

Without a table and a chair, and with papers smuggled in,

this book in your hands was conceived and drafted on my laps. Here in prison, chairs, tables, beds are a luxury. There may be times when value in a piece of work like this could be seen in the thought provoking subject matter, sincerity, circumstance and intention of the author rather than in the title, gold-rimmed cover of the book, international-acclaimed status of the author, quality and volume of the work alone.

That this small contribution to knowledge is made available for your reflection is proof of the fact that while in prison, it was my physical being that was deprived of freedom, not my spirit, soul and mind. The real man in me suffered no disconnects with you, the larger Southern Cameroons society, and most especially the wretched of the earth and humanity in general. With resolve, prison life was made a retreat: morally, intellectually and spiritually. The future of our country and the destiny of our children preoccupied me. This reinforced my conviction and inspired me to think aloud by writing so that by this we may concert and in solidarity fight for the liberation of our country. This is a historic duty, and in human life, not so many are often entrusted with such a divine duty. God created man free and equal and to each people He ordained their homeland, their heritage which they must cherish and nourish and bequeath to their descendants in whole and better than they found it and never in pieces and worse than they got it from their own ancestors. In Proverbs 23:10, the Creator divinely commanded "Do not move an ancient boundary stone or encroach on the fields of the fatherless" (NIV).

In fighting for the restoration of the statehood and independence of the Southern Cameroons we are doing God's will and respecting and defending international law. The mission of the SCNC is to dispossess the annexationist and colonial occupier by defending the ancient boundary stone and bringing freedom to those in bondage and good hope to the hopeless Southern Cameroonians.

Stating here that with resolve I transformed prison detention into a retreat is not to say that it was painless. Whoever invented prison gave tyrants and totalitarian regimes the worst instrument for the decapitation of the human spirit and will, most especially those opposed to tyranny. Freedom fighters inescapably are bound to be the greatest enemies of tyrants just as tyranny is the greatest enemy of man and the divine will for man. Tyranny violates the normal flow and rhythm of natural justice within any given human society.

What make unjust imprisonment meaningless are the spirit and the indefatigable stand of the victim who defiles the enemy's purpose to subject the physical body and decapitate the man thus putting an end to such great show of force. Tyrants are intolerant of any kind of opposition, no matter how legitimate and legal it may be. It is the spirit that conquers and overcomes. Once the human spirit remains on the throne as ordained by the Creator, both the mind and physical or will power are charged to work for the triumph of goodness over evil. It is the human spirit that enables the inner man, the real being to rule, direct and condition the blooming of that which is good, righteous and excellent. It is by standing up against injustice without relenting, without giving up, and retreating that the spine of tyranny is broken.

What matters in human life is not the immediate, but that which transcends: it is the long term effect of any single act of man, indeed how it impacts society and humanity in general. The triumph of the human spirit or good over evil, in this respect is not to say that once incarcerated behind the iron curtains and you are completely at the mercy of your captors and sometimes left there to rot away, your strong spirit does not make you suffer physical, psychological, moral pain. In fact the oppressor keeps you behind bars to break the spirit, decapitate the physical body and destroy the mind. How the spirit takes it makes the big difference. When in the face of all odds you do not bow, you do not retreat and you do not on your knees plead for mercy, you do not compromise, and you remain firm and refuse to surrender, it is the spirit on the throne leading you to defeat the arch enemy of man, namely, tyranny and gross injustice. When the spirit triumphs the oppressor is the vanquished and you the victor. This is the motive force and engine of human progress.

Change in society does not come by itself. It comes by hard work, sacrifice and the systematic defence of that which is lofty and righteous.

The take home message is: while the dictator is a symbol of evil, you as the defender of the ideal for man are the motive force of the human spirit reaching out for the possible best for man. Standing for human freedom, justice, progress and happiness, the values you enunciate are cardinal and cannot be blocked by any earthly force. While those who stand for a better world and greater humanity in dignity and the ideals they fight for will be remembered forever, the tyrant and the evil system he incarnates will be forgotten in the ashes of history. We live not in days but in deeds. But every tyrant is like an armed robber who refuses to learn from the one caught and tied to the stake for execution for his heinous crimes against humanity. The match for a better world and better humanity is an unstoppable phenomenon in the history of humankind. Southern Cameroons and Southern Cameroonians must be part and parcel of this better world and greater humanity by fighting for justice, legality, their freedom, equality, prosperity and dignity. They must stand for and forever defend the TRUTH and the divine will for man- born free and equal: none born in chains and poor or wretched and none born free and with gold and diamonds in his hands. God's endowment is to be exploited and used judiciously for the good of all mankind. And to surrender to annexation and foreign domination and alien rule and in perpetuity live in servitude is to betray God's infinite wisdom for creating you in his image. To stand by and lift no finger against this monster that dehumanises man is to betray the divine will for man.

When devil-inspired terror knows no limits

Captain Ahidjo in Kumbo, Bui County teaching Anglofools the unforgettable lesson, October 1, 2001

Bel Suika, one of victims of Capt. Ahidjo's mortal bullets, Kumbo, Bui County, October 1, 2001

Released SCNC LEADERS pay respect to the martyrs of October 1, 2001, in Bui County

2

Difficult to Believe

Overwhelmed with the determination and enthusiasm of the crowds pouring on the Commercial Avenue for the historic moment from different parts of Bamenda City my wife Mary Nan Nfor phoned and told me. "You people come out! It is now or never!!" I communicated this to our National Chairman, Dr. Luma. This good news energised and put a new lease of life in us the leaders and we got ready. Soon our signal man appeared with the vehicle to convey us from our hideout to the Commercial Avenue for the long awaited moment.

As we appeared the strategic leaders on the ground, Zachs Ndimongori, Fidelis Chinkwo, Mrs Regina Mankefor, signalled and the crowd in unison swung forward. As agreed, Dr. Martin Luma, the National Chairman, took position as the National Anthem, "Freedom Land", was solemnly sung. This attracted more people. Immediately the anthem was over the National Chairman started reading the anniversary speech. He did not finish when the reinforced occupation forces descended on us with extreme brutality and savagery. We kept our peace as we were being brutalized and arbitrarily arrested at gun point.

For being arrested, Frida Epusi who had sneaked away accused my wife of forcing us to get out and be arrested. She made it look like Mary Nan Nfor's husband was safe and enjoying the comfort of his home with the family. The manner in which this Frida Epusi had all along glued herself to our National Chairman was worrisome and disturbing to us. Though this Frida Epusi was Bakweri, and we never had any knowledge of blood relationship, she was not the wife of our Chairman. But she deprived us, SCNC leaders, even of privacy with our leader, a thing Mrs. Luma never did. This constituted not only cause for concern but solid grounds for genuine suspicion. Though not a leader she wanted to be part of and hear everything we had to discuss with our Chairman. Some of us suspected her of sinister intentions. But our warnings to our National Chairman did not yield fruit. We were finally proven damn right.

After our brutal arrest, torture and detention, the conspicuous absence of Mr. A F. Ndangam both at the Commercial Avenue and non-arrest as others were picked up after including Francis Ade, the National Treasurer, became a matter of big concern to many. Mr. Vincent Feko, the Secretary General couldn't hold his peace. In prison detention days passed without us seeing him though tension in the town and all over North West was however still very high. While we were underground he was not with us. As Chair of Foreign Affairs Commission with computer facilities he, Mr. Ndangam was our window on the wall with the larger world. So that morning of 1st October, 2001 he came with copy of the anniversary speech for the National Chairman, Dr. Luma, and took excuse and returned to fax copies to the UNSG and other world leaders. As we prayerfully waited for the population to gather and signal for us to come, he never re-joined us. At the Commercial Avenue there was no sign of him. Consistent with our Gandhian philosophy, as brutal as the forces descended on us, we never fought back, we offered no resistance. Having concretely made the point and presented the anniversary speech we were satisfied. As for weapons of brutalization and termination of human life, we were unarmed. None had even a stick or stone. But we were well armed with truth, legitimacy and legality which promote human dignity, the equality of all nations, big and small and world peace based on justice. These universal values which we incarnate and defend even the colonizer cannot brush aside.

But Frida Ngwa who seems to have come as Dr. Arnold Yonbang's SCARM representative couldn't bear the brutality of the forces. She fought back to the embarrassment of the Francophone gendarmes and police. Summoning the last atom of energy in her, she fought two officers like a wounded lion. And to overcome the humiliation this Graffi woman was out to subject them to, they kicked her mercilessly with their heavy boots and she sauntered to the ground and was carried and dumped into their truck.

Scared by the brutality of the armed troops that memorable 1st October 2001, Theodore Leke, who stood to my right, like a fly disappeared into thin air! Throughout our detention we never saw him come to visit us nor did we get word from him. He was busy enjoying his quiet life with the CDC where he worked.

At GMI, we were all packed in one small room with our lone female compatriot. It was so trying a moment as we all had only a bucket well positioned at a corner as our toilet. Under such inhuman degrading circumstances it is not natural even for a man to feel like making water not to talk less of a lone woman among more than fifteen men. In my deep conscience I couldn't bear the sight of Frida Ngwa as she squatted on the floor at the other end of the room. I felt for her, as helpless as I was. Such psychological torture inflicted severer pain than what we suffered at the Commercial Avenue. It was big relief when she was called out late at night and taken to another room. The effect of her brutal torture and hard kicks on her stomach became so severe while in prison detention and she had to be admitted at the Bamenda Provincial hospital for treatment. She should be remembered not just for being the lone lady arrested on Oct. 1st 2001. She should equally and significantly be remembered for her courage that she stood firm and fought back while some men cowardly fled and never looked back. She was the Queen Esther of 2001. She ably represented the British Southern Cameroons mother for the new dawn.

Unlike the Black Saturday in Ndu of June 6th 1992 where men and women detained in a classroom at the Ndu Commercial College were forced to strip naked, sit with legs wide open facing the opposite sex, we were spared such dehumanising treatment. This is the sad experience of three-month pregnant Madame Florence Yaya as recorded in 'NAKED TRUTH ABOUT THAT NDU GENOCIDE, 1995 p.27', quote:

> "Because I was about three months pregnant, it was difficult for me to open my legs as wide as they needed. At this, I was kicked with the boots on the back and one gendarme told me to open my mouth very wide. He then gave me three strokes on the face with the rubber truncheon while I fell (down) unconscious."

Though admitted and treated at Ndu Baptist Health Centre next day of pains sustained from the hard kicks on her back, the pains persisted and two months after the incident, she had miscarriage of a set of twins (male and female).

One embarrassing experience at GMI where we spent the first night after transfer from the Public Security was the queer behaviour of a police officer may be related to Mr. Vincent Feko. Quite early in the morning, this gentleman opened the door gently and entered. It was then we knew that the door could be opened and closed without the revolting and ear splitting noise. With his back firmly on the door, he burst into tears pleading with Feko, our SG "You should leave this thing!" Subbing relentlessly like a kitten, he continued "Do you want to die like Titahunjio? Leave this thing! I say leave this thing!! Leave this your thing!!!" And the deluge flew down profusely as if to hastily empty what he had preserved for this purpose before he could be discovered. And he wiped his eyes quickly and stealthily moved out and banged the door in its designed revolting manner.

His mention of Titahunjio, murdered in Bafoussam detention, was a painful reminder to us all. A fine gentleman well brought up and professionally trained teacher and real patriot of the struggle for freedom and justice for his people and nation, his valid contributions for a better fatherland were brutally terminated in the most barbaric manner in Bafoussam, la République du Cameroun, where he was kidnapped to from Ndop where he had been arbitrarily arrested.

But who was the criminal? Was it the murderers or the murdered? This is how a slave who refuses to defend his true identity and self-worth and fight for his inherent rights blames those who summon courage to do the right thing behaves. As he spoke, neither his concerned man, Feko, whom in the characteristic nature of the coloniser's policy of divide and rule he wanted to isolate from among us nor any of us uttered a word. Throughout our prison detention life we saw more of such acts of efforts to isolate one from among us or the divide and rule tactics to weaken us. The behaviour of this Southern Cameroons lackey police officer was a shocking encounter to all of us in an early morning in a detention cell. I have never seen a man with such a deluge of tears to shed within such a limited space of time. The man in him was long dead and forgotten. He was a moving corps and as Christ said of Judas Iscariot, it were better this man were not born.

We noticed that he rushed quite early to deliver his uncalled for message to avoid being seen by any of his francophone bosses and be accused of collaborating with "subversive elements". Such a link could cost him long term imprisonment and/or instant dismissal for such an unpardonable crime. Every francophone in the force, even a recruit, is a boss to every Anglofool (Southern Cameroonian) in the force, thanks to the former's proximity to the authorities and this they freely exploit at will. All power, political, economic, military, and judicial, is monopolized by the francophones and Southern Cameroonians being the subjugated are watched and held in suspicion. Even the most loyal Southern Cameroonian worshipper of the Yaoundé high apostle, who to some is a demi god, is not trusted.

As painful as it is, it is absolutely necessary that I make a statement or two on the arbitrary arrest, torture and detention of Titahunjio in Ndop, where he was teaching and kidnap to Bafoussam, la République du Cameroun, where he met his death in the hands of his merciless torturers. The invasion of his compound in the dead of the night by armed troops and final torture to death in prison detention in Bafoussam can only be compared with the mercilessness of apartheid police in South Africa. If Titahunjio committed a crime in Ndop, where he was living and working, what law justified his being kidnapped and detained in Bafoussam, la République du

Cameroun?

After his cruel murder we made efforts with the Human Rights Defense Group (HRDG) for justice to take its course. But the Ndop occupation forces intimidated and harassed the family assuring them that any who cooperated with us was going to suffer the very fate of Titahunjio. Consequently the two wives and numerous children he left behind have had to live in poverty, constant insecurity, fear and psychological torture. Most painfully, here the widows are subjected to physical, moral, spiritual and psychological torture as they are made to bear the burden of the loss of their beloved husbands without the right to express the anguish by mourning. This is a painful trauma a widow is forced to bear for in mourning a widow shares the burden with other family members and friends and this reduces the weight of loss. When gendarmes in brutal style disrupt the traditional mourning system, they deprive the bereaved family, most especially the widow, of the traditional social and moral obligations, indeed an established-honoured social contract, others have towards her. So as it was with the Titahunjio widows, so has it been with the widow of George Shinyuy and many others. What a burdensome scar to live with to your own death!

During our prison detention the behaviour of A. F. Ndangam, Theodore Leke and James Sabum became an issue. Our S.G. Vincent Feko was indeed bitter about such suspicious behaviour of these gentlemen. As Chairman of Foreign Affairs Commission and former Vice Chairman to National Chairman, Bar. Sam E. Elad, Ndangam was without doubt a high ranking and respectable official of the movement. While Leke and Sabum came from outside Bamenda, Ndangam was with us throughout and participated in all arrangements and decisions arrived at. To Vincent Feko and others, his absence at Commercial Avenue, which they found inadmissible, wasn't an accident of history.

Their anger and disappointment had a solid base. To calm down nerves I argued that if all of us were behind bars with none outside to keep the flames of the struggle alive, it would be counterproductive. And that our prayer should be that those leaders outside should be positively active. This may be termed damage control but I was not in the least being the devil's advocate. Our National Chairman, Dr. Luma called for calm and that this was not the time for negative remarks about anyone but to consolidate team spirit. True to point, Mr. Ndangam as Chair of Foreign Affairs Commission produced a comprehensive report on the Commemoration of the 40th anniversary of the confiscation of Southern Cameroons independence by la République du Cameroun, the brutal killings, maiming and arrests and detention in different towns. This report received worldwide circulation and without doubt accounted for the attention and visits even from abroad, which our detention attracted.

SCNC Leaders in Bamenda Central Prison, Standing, (L-R) Sona, Nfor, Ade Francis, Pa Ndi, Feko, Luma, Chief Ayamba, Mbinglo. In front (L-R) Pa Nya, & Nwachan

3

The Real World of Bamenda Central Prison

As I experienced it, the prison is quite a world of its own. It is jungle kingdom where anarchy is the constitution. Quite often people struggling to lead talk of change. But most often much of what they talk of are things and situations they have heard of or what they imagine and not what they have lived or personally experienced. This is why post-colonial African leaders such as Kwame Nkrumah of Ghana, Jomo Kenyatta of Kenya, Nelson Mandela of South Africa, among others, are in a class of their own as contrasted with the likes of Ahidjo, Bokassa, Mobutu, and the rest, tyrants who were brought in by the colonial masters as their heirs to serve colonial interest.

What is today known as Bamenda Central Prison was established by colonial administration for all of present day Northern Zone made up of seven Counties, (divisions). Under the Southern Cameroons the place had facilities for training of inmates in various skills to be useful citizens upon leaving the prison yard. There was no overcrowding and inmates were well cared for and sure of three good meals a day. They had their uniform and looked neat always. The prison environment with lawns was clean; paths were cemented and adorned with flowers. There was discipline and order.

But today, like all other institutions inherited by Yaoundé, Bamenda Central Prison stands in ruins. Buildings are dilapidated and in need of urgent repairs. The left over small patches of cement and stones that separated the cemented foot paths from flower beds are visible everywhere. The well-kept lawns of yesterday have disappeared giving way to dust everywhere in the dry season and mud in the rainy season. As you stumble on one or the other, you are angrily reminded of the good old days of Bamenda Prison.

Are we a cursed generation? Have the gods of the land gotten angry, so angry and abandoned the people to their man-made fate?

In the Bamenda Central Prison we did not only see inmates suffering, on arrival we lived the worse. Our cell was a newly constructed building just cemented and painted, thanks to a philanthropic organisation that came to the rescue of inmates suffocating from overcrowding. Both the walls and the floor of the building were still wet when we were brought in that night.

This was our second transfer, first from Public Security to the dreaded GMI, and from GMI to Prison detention. Each transfer was at night and gave the oppressive police the opportunity to demonstrate their brutality and inhumanity. First the deafening opening of the iron door, Gbang! Gbang! Gbang! Then Gbraaaang! Just the loud banging and opening of the door alone was a revolting reminder that you were as powerless as a caged rat! After the ear-splitting noise of opening the door come the authoritarian announcement, "come out!" That is if you were lucky to have an Anglofool bold enough to give the instructions in English. French was the language of the Master, the language of authority and command.

With aggressively looking police lined up with fingers on the trigger we were matched to the awaiting truck. As the noisy truck started ascending the Up Station hill driven so aggressively, with no right even to whisper to your colleague, our thoughts went wild. Are we on our long trip to the dreaded Kondengui maximum prison, Yaoundé? Once a captive your life is in your captor's hands. Your life hangs on a pendulum, swung so aggressively by the "master" who has the bits of your life in his palms. Until we reached the Bamenda Central Prison, we knew not where we were being ferried to. That is part of the psychological torture. You know not and you have not today or tomorrow. Your captors are so arrogant that they discuss nothing with you but shout commands at you. So you have no right to know what next.

This building was not yet electrified; so we lived in darkness for the first few days. Our first pre occupation was to use toilet roll, rags and even our clothes to reduce the amount of water on the floor in order to squat or lie on the bare wet and cold cement floor. Mr Vincent Feko, the SCNC Secretary General, who had lived under regular high temperatures in Douala for years, caught a severe cold and was shaking like a lily in troubled waters. Were it not for additional coats that he was given, the story the next day could have sometimes been a bad one; worse in enemy camp whose aggressive arrogant bosses cared less about our safety, security and comfort. It would have been double tragedy for us in enemy camp. With our deplorable condition in the cell, we had cause to fear for the worse and as we prayed, God answered our prayers.

The situation was so bad that I forgot about myself and was concerned about the octogenarians, three in number, in our group. These were Pa Stephen Ndi, Chief Ayamba, and Dr Martin N. Luma, our National Chairman. The latter's case was most pitiable. In addition to his height and age, he had a broken leg whose burden weight he was condemned to nurse and end his life with here on earth. Despite his walking stick we had to help him sit down or stand up each time. We had to protest vigorously before we were allowed to bring in mattresses from our homes and a contractor sympathiser gave us some two short benches. That no one from our group died of pneumonia or some other disease, God our creator alone can explain how He did save us.

The inhuman treatment we were subjected to and the deplorable and squalid conditions we lived in vividly remind me of Nelson Mandela's prison condition in apartheid South Africa. As recorded in his book, 'The Long Walk to Freedom", he was given two light blankets while in prison. He and his ANC colleagues were given beds and regularly given good food. Albert Mukong in the days of Ahmadou Ahidjo at the Mantoum Concentration Camp was given a "vono bed and a mattress". But here we were not yet charged, tried, let alone condemned to any terms of imprisonment, treated worse than a black man condemned to life imprisonment under South African apartheid rule. Yet we all know and condemn apartheid, the Yaoundé regime inclusive, as the worst oppressive system that has ever been imposed on a people on this planet earth. This despicable inhuman treatment we were forced to endure can make someone conclude that comparatively Mandela lived in a hotel while in Robben Island prison in South Africa. This tells you the evil inherent in neo-apartheid.

By right we were political prisoners fighting against a colonial regime as such entitled to respectable treatment. But here we were being treated worse than murderers and armed robbers in our own land by a foreign occupying regime.

But what pushes other human beings to descend to such instinctive behaviour and acts of bestiality against other human beings? If the chief Prison Administrator, Mr Mbarga and his francophone arrogant administrators were of a different colour, one would rightly have accused them of racism. Brain washed and fed with the notion that Bamenda, in particular, and Southern Cameroons in general, was enemy territory where the people are hostile, are the hard core enemies of the state, they the defenders of the Yaoundé regime were posted on special mission to crack down on the enemy. Natured to believe that the survival of the state was predicated on the survival of the incumbent leader, any change was thus intolerable and unacceptable to those who benefitted from the evil system. The enemies of the state must of necessity be eliminated.

As if this dehumanising treatment in the hands of our oppressors and captors was not severe enough, a plague – "*kritchiser*", as I christen it, left its marks on each of us. *Kritchiser* is a skin disease caused by a tiny black insect commonly known as "*kritchi*". The tiny insects were attracted by electric light brought into the cell after we complained of living in darkness. The insects invaded our two cells and we relentlessly waged a war against them. Each morning after battling throughout the night, it was fun fighting the invaders on the white walls and sweeping them out. We then examined the new victims and the affected parts of the face, neck, armpit, among others. Our handy medicine was toothpaste which we faithfully robed on the affected parts of the body.

I can't remember who prescribed toothpaste as medicine or who started using it as such. But in our hopeless situation, faith in whatever thing worth doing was the basis for survival. With swollen painted parts of the face turning black, for example, *kritchiser* could deform you beyond recognition even by your wife and children. We were only saved after several weeks of suffering, when the contractor sealed the small holes, in the name of windows, some three and half metres up the walls.

While we received no preferential treatment from the colonial authorities to let even other prison inmates envy us, our detention soon transformed the Bamenda Central Prison into a holy shrine visited by both the believer and non-believer and the high and lowly. What made it spectacular was the fact that we were detainees for a people's cause, namely, freedom from annexation and foreign domination and alien rule. Many questions were being asked and answered. We became redeemers overnight; a sweet sounding title which no one, not even the oppressive Yaoundé regime could take away from us. The people had made and pronounced their judgement and so crowned us. Journalists made their rounds and the lawyers adorned the court with their robes. This being the first of its kind in the land, it was spectacular. Both the Central Prison and the Bamenda Courts where our matter was being handled became centres of attraction. At the court the police found it difficult to control the crowds.

This was not all. The longer we were kept behind the bar the more people visited the prison. What is popularly described as the Bamenda or Graffi hospitality assumed a different dimension with abundant food, fruits and other essentials brought in for our upkeep. We had humbly declined eating the terrible poor prison food. This was not just due to its terribly poor quality: there was more to our decision. With abundant good will from the population, we had more than enough food to spare. I believe this gave us excess energy that generated enough heat with which the wet walls and floors were forced to get dry quickly. The Bamenda population fought and sacrificed even more than we in prison sacrificed. The spectacular good work of the women, the "Takembeng" under the mobilising skilful Madam Regina Mankefor will ever be appreciated. God from his abundance will richly bless them.

Nfor N. Nfor & Pa Stephen Ndi, 78 veteran soldier of WWII, on bench in Bamenda central prison, 2001

4

Within the Iron Fence

Though this was not the first time I suffered arrest and detention for my political conviction and beliefs, all previous ones (five in all) were in gendarmerie and police cells. The time spent at the Central Prison, Bamenda, gave me an opportunity to live in the hell of the moral bankruptcy, unbridled corruption, bureaucratic bottle-necks, beyond pardon injustice, francophone bossy arrogance, discrimination, you name it. At the Bamenda Central Prison, the francophone Prison Administrator, Monsieur Fulbert MBARGA, was indeed the Lord of the manor and his word, law.

The prison, whose inmates range from people in their early teens to those above seventy, is a factory where amateur criminals go to become hardened criminals and drug addicts. Some teenage youths who were alleged to have stolen cups of garri, biscuits, soap or who, as sales boys accused of embezzlement by their employers were thrown in and forgotten, spent upwards of two to three years without a charge and trial. It is good business all the same for the boss of the prison and his collaborators while the victims languish.

The prison has no farm yet every early morning prisoners bring in wood and bitter leaf. From where do they get bitter leaf and wood other than stealing from people's farms? They have a meal of poorly cooked corn fufu with bitter leaf whose only ingredient is salt every day. With this malnutrition was rife. Some who could not have assistance from relations or friends either due to long and difficult distances or hardship found it difficult to survive. Some were mere skeletons with scabies all over the body. Some could not help picking banana peels to feed on. Our door became a shrine for hope. Is it that the Yaoundé government never allocates funds for their feeding and upkeep?

Worse of all assistance brought in by philanthropic bodies if not supervised closely by the donor disappears into individual houses of prison administrators. Prisoners living the hopeless lives of captives have no rights so they watch in unbelief how help brought to them disappear for the benefit of those who have. It was as if these prison administrators were graduates of special imperial seminaries where only one verse from the entire holy book Matthew 25:29 (KJV) "For unto every one that hath shall be given, and he shall have abundance: but from him that hath not shall be taken away even that which he hath," is rigorously taught for faithful implementation and self-aggrandisement in Southern Cameroons. With no rights to be heard, to whom can they the prisoners complain? They are to be seen but never to be heard let alone respected.

Those in Awaiting Trial (AT) are in hell on earth. For any that has been here to go to hell again after death, this will amount to living in hell twice, first in Southern Cameroons prison under la République du Cameroun, and second in Satan's lake of hell fire in the hereafter.

Here I saw quite a lot of prison inmates with chains of varied degrees on their feet. Recalling my first encounter with prisoners at the Buea Prison, (in the days of West Cameroon and the lame-legged Federal Republic of Cameroon) while a student at the Baptist Teachers Training College (BTTC) Soppo, Buea, I concluded that those in chains were those condemned to death. But I could not understand why the chains were not the same as those I saw in the then Buea

Prison and why they were so many inmates in chains. Some of those in chains were teenagers. Could these youths be murderers sentenced to death? This further worried me. If teenagers of such tender ages could be murderers condemned to death, then the society was not only irredeemably morally and spiritually bankrupt, it was as rotten as a rotten egg, I mournfully concluded.

Unlike in the past when the legacy of the Anglo-Saxon system was still in force, Prisoners are used by some Warders to generate income for themselves (the Warders). In addition to having them work in their residences, as if house boys or work as labourers in towns on some paid projects with incomes going to the "big men of the prison," a prisoner could be in chains for a defined sum of money. As he pays in bits the chain is relaxed until the whole sum is paid. But in case he fails to pay his feet remain chained, or the chain could even be fastened so that the individual jumps with the two feet as a frog instead of walking. Such inhuman treatment confined and restricted the movement of the individual even in prison. But the authorities called this "discipline" as if imprisonment under such inhuman conditions was not punishment enough.

The francophone warders were exceptionally hard and merciless on prisoners. The least excuse gave them free latitude to demonstrate their mission in Southern Cameroons.

To get their understanding so that we feed the prisoners on the danger list, which I gathered due to starvation and under nourishment, it was imperative that we give the Warders their own share. Thus you beg or even go to the extent of bribing to feed the hungry and the under nourished. This "understanding" obtained, we did the best that we could. We soon saw improvement on the faces of those in the AT I had on the danger list. Here to be in log ahead with Warders is digging your grave with your elbows, as the Wimbum proverb states. By their attitude they cannot be loved and respected by prisoners. But you can't ignore them. And you can't do without them either. Circumstances force you to tolerate them by pretending to respect them in order to survive and avoid further degradation. Behind these cold solitary walls you are at their mercy.

While deprived of our liberty, on the instructions of the proconsuls, the Legal Department charged us in court. Avoiding the real issue, namely, "secession" or "treason," as was first threateningly pronounced to us, we were accused of violating a Prefectoral Order and disrupting public peace. The so-called Prefectoral Order was signed by Mr Charles Nzege, a Southern Cameroonian lackey on the instructions of his francophone Proconsul - Governor Adrien Kouambo, days after our arrest and detention. To cover up, as usual, it was backdated. For his reward for being a "good boy", he, Charles Nzege, was appointed Governor in Buea even before we were released. The following year Kouambo himself was appointed Minister. In Southern Cameroons it has thus become an established fact, indeed an unwritten law, that the more the proconsul suppress, maim or even eliminate the subjugated people, the surer the chances of his appointment to a higher post. Fear and terror must reign to keep the annexed people subservient. This, the occupier of our land calls the "reign of peace" and demands motions of support from the lackeys on their knees begging for higher appointment or conscience money.

The courts went into the matter. Our defending lawyers filed an application for Habeas Corpus and bail. This gave us a lot of hope. But at first and on instructions of the proconsuls we were not brought to court. Each day the case was up for hearing, the Bamenda population turned out heavily with some coming from as far as Donga Mantung, Meme, Fako, Bui etc. After several hearings, the court granted bail on grounds that our arrests and detention were illegal. The first time it was ignored by proconsuls and Prison Director. Suppressed anger and frustration in some among us rose and was self-evident. Our lawyers took an appeal to the High Court. The High Court, after examining the matter and respecting the Anglo-Saxon Common Law system, upheld the judgment of the lower court. All three bails granted were ignored with impunity by the proconsuls who owe their positions to Mr Biya. We were even threatened that any protest, even by Southern Cameroonians in town, will worsen our condition.

But surprisingly at about 19.30pm Cameroon time on November 17 2001, Mr Mbarga, accompanied by two other francophone prison authorities, ignoring his vice, Mr Francis Ngwayu, a Southern Cameroonian, bounced in and gave us what amounted to a scolding and a lecture fit for pre adolescents who know not their rights. At the end he told us we were released and we should leave immediately.

In my capacity as the National Vice Chairman and speaking on behalf of my colleagues and our leader Dr Martin Luma, who was sick in the Prison Clinic, I told him to inform the Governor that we were going to confer and give a reply to his matching orders the following morning. He was told in clear language that we could not leave under the cover of darkness.

While I stood defending this position, Francis Ade, to the embarrassment of every one among us, picked his bag and bolted out. But every other person stood still without moving.

Before coming they had put off the light in our apartment. At this time, as usual, all other prison cells were safely and securely lucked from outside. This was a task dutifully implemented every 18.00 hours Cameroon time daily, whatever may be the situation. So whatever happened to us no other prisoner would have had the privilege of witnessing or even hearing. They were by order sealed off.

Our defiant reply gave Mbarga and his lieutenants the greatest shock of their life. How do these "Anglo fools" disobey the instructions of the Governor, they must have pondered. Since orders must be executed, he had to bring in more warders who used force to get us out. So we left without signing the usual discharge papers and our few belongings which were collected the following day. It was external pressure, which made Mr Biya to issue matching orders to his subordinates to release us. That night, it was Mr Kouambo, the Governor, and the Prison Director, Mbarga, got us out and save their high posts or a nod of the Presidential head could cost them their prestigious positions in la République du Cameroun's colony, the Southern Cameroons, if we failed leaving.

Our unexpected release after rejecting bails with impunity was not unprecedented. At the end of December 1992 the release of Justice Nyo Wakai (rtd) and 172 others took everyone by surprise. But as nothing is hidden under the sun, their release was based on firm instructions from President Paul Biya who on return from his usual flamboyant and most expensive trips to Europe instructed that the 173 Anglofools should be out of Yaoundé before 1993 New Year day. This is what it takes to be the Commander-in-Chief and Chief Magistrate. His orders are cut in the rock and must be obeyed and executed.

To prove that within the Central Prison the word of the Director, was the never - bending law, as the word of the colonial Proconsul was the imperial edict in the province, Mr Mbarga reinforced the team with clear instructions to use force and get us out. While he prepared for this, with the help of a torch, thanks to Chief Ayamba, I used the mobile phone, I had concealed and contacted our able Lawyer, Harmony Bobga, our Iron Lady, Madam Regina Mankefor to mobilise the population and come up with vehicles and convey us down town. This was necessary to guarantee our safety and security, because the enemy could sponsor agents to ambush and eliminate us and claim that our death took place out of prison and their jurisdiction.

To attain our desired objective, we spent enough time arguing and resisting even their use of force. In the circumstance and unknown to the enemy, a sizeable population gathered in front of the Bamenda Central Prison. Flooded by women, it was like a "cry-die" and the women noisily accused them of every imaginable evil. This reminded them of an incidence one evening some three weeks back when, like wild fire, rumour spread that, as happened in 1992 and 1997, we were, like captives, to be transferred to the dreaded Kondengui prison, Yaoundé, la République du Cameroun. The Takembeng and the Bamenda women, under Madam Mankefor camped in front of the Prison and refused leaving even after every assurance was given that there was no such intention to transfer us. They only left when we appealed to them assuring them that at the slightest sensing of any funny game they would be contacted immediately.

To challenge a Bamenda woman with the extermination of the life of her child makes her wilder than a wounded lion. Show her love, respect, you see the angel and god-likeness in this God's creature. But the least evil intention, you are bound to see the wounded lion in her. Love and self-preservation is her greatest gift from the Most High.

With this meaningful effort, we left Bamenda Central Prison that night as victors with a jubilant crowd in organised vehicles that ensured our safety and security down town. We moved straight and took camp at Barrister H. Bobga's Chambers where we the released detainees spent the night. About 10.00am next morning, thanks to our Lawyer's advice, contacts were made and we granted a Press Conference to announce to our fellow compatriots and the world the circumstances of our unconventional release. In the Press Conference we thanked all for their support, reaffirmed our total commitment to the struggle and called on our compatriots to remain steadfast to the end and assured them that the SCNC, like the ANC of South Africa, will win the war against annexation, colonial occupation, neo-apartheid and bring freedom, human dignity, progress and sovereign independence to the British Southern Cameroons.

After the Press Conference we resolved to make a pilgrimage to Bui County to honour the compatriots murdered by the coloniser of our land on 1st October, 2001. They paid the supreme prize and their blood watered the tree of freedom. In African tradition it was necessary we condone and share the burden of loss with the respective families. In Bui we also made a courtesy call on H.R. Fon Mbinglo, the Natural Ruler of Nso. While in Bui it turned out to be a hilarious welcome of victors, indeed a triumphant entry into Jerusalem of the saviour and liberator of the down trodden and those heavily burdened with the yoke of annexation, neo-apartheid, colonial occupation, foreign domination and alien rule in the third millennium.

Court Hall & yard filled with SCNC activists listening to trial of their leaders, Bamenda, 2001

5

The Bitter-Sweet

Circumstances of our arbitrary arrest notwithstanding, none of us could have imagined that we were to be kept in solitary confinement for more than a couple of days. This vain wish was strengthened when the matter was taken to court and our lawyers applied for bail. Among us were some who had never experienced torture, arbitrary arrest, let alone detention under life-threatening circumstances. From their behaviour and eagerness to compromise they constituted a big embarrassment to some of us.

We saw the need and urgency to establish some order, discipline, group decorum and responsibility as a solid team with a mission under recognised leadership. Firstly we had to adopt a clear position and solid stand as SCNC leaders and activists defending our right to self- determination. Secondly, we had to adopt and hold as an article of faith that as Southern Cameroonians we violated no law of la République du Cameroun by commemorating our independence day in our land. This was necessary for contradictory behaviour and statements from any could terribly be counterproductive.

In spite of this basic agreement some dangerous cracks soon surfaced in our midst. We had all agreed that we should rise or fall like one man. But soon there was some move from Lawyer Sama Francis to handle Francis Ade's case separately. Francis Ade, the National Treasurer, was a high ranking official of the SCNC. Though he had not been with us when we went underground and at the Commercial Avenue where the National Chairman, Dr. Martin N. Luma gave the historic

40th anniversary speech to the population, he was however, like many others, arrested in town and joined with us. This move coming from the SDF Lawyer on grounds that Francis Ade was equally an SDF Councillor for Bamenda Council was a bitter pill to swallow. We vehemently protested. Though they did not insist, our reasoned protest, without doubt was an embarrassment to the SDF leadership. This victory registered notwithstanding, it became self-evident that his wife and family, with evident tacit support and urgings from Ade himself, continued underground moves to get him out, sooner than later.

As the days rolled by and granted bails by the court were over-ruled by the colonial administration, it became clear that we were to be in for some long stay. With no sign in the horizon it was evident that our release was indefinite. This called for adjustment and accepting what could not be changed.

Through visits by individuals, groups, nationals and foreigners, especially religious groups, we soon had enough bibles and spiritual instruction materials. Enough time was devoted to spiritual nourishment and seeking God's favour and intervention. Mr Thomas Nwachan automatically became our pastor and was known as such. He did not only handle sermons, he also became a Joseph of the bible who could interpret dreams.

Morning and evening devotion was regular. Spiced with lively singing of favourite choruses and sometimes dancing, this became both a moral, spiritual, intellectual and even physical tonic. Thomas Nwachan, our confessed pastor, was good at intoning the choruses though some of us occasionally came in with some. Some of his most favourite choruses were "My Lord you are worthy, worthy to be praised" and "Prayer is the key. Prayer is the master key." Being an SCNC assembly "Courage brothers do not stumble", which was the theme sung in Buea 1993 at the birth of the SCNC could not be left out. This fired the spirit for solidarity assuring us of eminent victory.

Equating our arbitrary arrest and detention with that of Paul and Silas by the imperial Roman Government, this chorus:

When Paul and Silas were praising the Lord, (2)
The Holy Ghost came down
Paul and Silas
They prayed, they sang
The Holy Ghost came down

He delivered Paul and Silas, (2)
My God delivered Paul and Silas
He will surely deliver me, (us)
 (What about you? Or us?)

This became another favourite song most especially when bail was turned down for the third time by the proconsuls.

After morning devotion we would anxiously listen to any dreamer narrate his dream for our "Joseph" to interpret. Favourite dreams centred around snakes and some bad creatures, someone wrestling victorious or wining in a race, someone dreaming of having some celebration or having a good time with family or friends, among others.

Our Joseph would sometimes quote verses from the scriptures to substantiate his interpretation.

In any dream involving the snake or the devil this was likened to the Yaoundé regime symbolised by President Biya and his gendarmes. As the head of the snake has to be crushed so shall the Yaoundé evil regime be defeated and Southern Cameroons triumph in its legitimate and legal quest for freedom and independence. Dreams about celebration were interpreted as a direct pointer to SCNC victory.

Such positive interpretation after morning devotion and before breakfast was a social, moral, intellectual, and spiritual tonic. They brightened the day giving hope of better things to come. Such were constant reminders of Paul and Silas imprisoned for preaching the message of truth, salvation, deliverance from bondage and how they were finally set free. Above all the victory dreams gave us courage and reassured us that lies and falsehood have never triumphed over truth nor has evil ever triumphed over goodness and gross injustice over justice. The truth must always prevail!

Such sparkling assurance always took us further removing any doubts and generating great hope. Joseph of the bible left prison after interpreting King Pharaoh's dream to become the Governor of Egypt. He later saved his own kind from crushing famine. And, in Africa, Kwame Nkrumah left prison to become Prime Minister of the Gold Coast and finally President of independent Ghana. As a great visionary he championed the birth of the Organisation of African Unity, the forerunner of African Union. And most recently, Nelson Mandela, the great son of Africa, left prison after twenty seven years to become President of South Africa. He defeated the worst form of foreign rule and alien domination known in human history, namely, apartheid.

With this and further nourished by Romans 5:3-5 which states:

> "…we also rejoice in our suffering, because we know

that suffering produces perseverance, perseverance, character; and character, hope. And hope does not disappoint us because God has poured out his love into our hearts by the Holy Spirit whom he has given us." (From the NIV Bible)

We remained confident that we were going to triumph irrespective of the odds. We were constantly cheered by the hope of victory to be.

Such concrete evidence of victory over evil and where men, though unjustly imprisoned, remained steadfast and focused; such evidence inspired and emboldened us. These men overcame evil and injustice not for themselves but for humanity. They have left eternal enviable lessons for human kind that to compromise and submit to foreign domination and alien rule is treachery. In this light we saw ourselves as pace setters and agents of the new dawn bound to come. After all, the tyrant, no matter how powerful he may be, is never forever invulnerable.

Morning devotion and dream interpretation came to stand in our prison life as sunshine and brightness cheering up the weak. For those who had bad nights this dispelled the sad memories and to us all such sharing in communal love engineered warmth and a new lease of life in us all.

Thomas Nwachan's role as pastor did not just stop at preaching and being Joseph the dream interpreter. As for preaching and praying, some of us shared in playing this role.

One morning he decided to move one step up the rung of his pastoral role. He decided to offer the Lord's Supper. Having resigned ourselves to fate and making the best use of the circumstances we saw nothing wrong, abnormal or funny about his playing this unique role. Here, in the SCNC assembly worship, there was no distinction between Catholic and Protestant, so no one questioned or insisted that it should be called one thing or the other. We just accepted it and collectively went along. With available bread and some Top, he administered the Lord's Super. This may be offering a lesson, and why not a challenge, to the Pastors and Reverend gentlemen to consider fulfilling this aspect of our Christian life to our fellow brothers and sisters behind the iron fence. Not too long after this solemn ceremony, our unexpected unceremonious release, as recorded above, came.

6

Through The Eye of Prison Detention

Prison became a school both for our spiritual growth, political education, social and moral edification, sound knowledge about the history of our nation and the legality and legitimacy of the struggle in fulfilment of our inherent and inalienable right to self-determination and in conformity with the UN Charter. This went on first among ourselves and secondly among other inmates to whom we had become a special class of detainees or prisoners. To those who knew nothing or little about the SCNC struggle and the younger generation who knew nothing about the British Southern Cameroons and the distinct identities of the two Cameroons, the message of liberation was the message of their political salvation.

To those who had spent many years in AT without a charge and whose accusers were satisfied with having dumped them in prison, it was relieving message to learn of the good old days of the defunct British Southern Cameroons. To them the bitterness against gendarmes only increased and fuelled heightened hatred when they learnt that in the then British Southern Cameroons there were no gendarmes and the police were friends not foe of the common man. They saw the extreme wickedness of the gendarme in the fact that he is the incarnation of foreign power. Not only did the gendarme represented foreign rule, the French language was also seen as an alien language and concrete evidence of foreign domination and alien rule for it was the language of the colonial oppressor. To those who had never known that in law and reality there were two distinct Cameroons, these youths then understood it in the existence of two foreign languages. They also learnt that in British Southern Cameroons the courts were independent of the executive and the law favoured the innocent and the prisons were not centres of torture and dehumanisation but centres of education, training in skills, correction, shaping and remoulding the character of those in society who had been misled by circumstances. Such lessons from us and what we did practically made them to long for the new dawn, where they would be masters of their own country and live in freedom, justice and equal opportunity for all the citizens.

With these facts and more they saw the stack differences between the two Cameroons and longed for peaceful separation and restoration of the British Southern Cameroons nation. Having lived under the states of emergency, the gendarme has always been the symbol of the reign of terror, a murderer, an extortionist, a rapist, and symbol of the evil regime in Yaoundé. To all these no sacrifice was too big to be made to get rid of the Yaoundé domination in British Southern Cameroons. These youths inspired by the hope of a better future, were eager for action to end the evil rule of Yaoundé. While the younger generation learnt of such good old days for their first time, the older generation in nostalgia be-mourned what the Southern Cameroonian people have lost in exchange for an evil, corrupt and repressive system. Until you love, cherish and long for what you have been forced to lose, you cannot vehemently hate what you have been forced to become and endure.

With our open arms to other prison inmates and warders, the gospel of the SCNC struggle soon had many converts and sympathisers in Bamenda Central Prison. We were not seen as criminals but freedom fighters for a better Southern Cameroons. We were loved and admired by those who believed in the legitimacy and legality of the struggle. Such wished they were part of us enjoying and sharing in such lavished sunshine of being redeemers of a people for a new dawn.

One afternoon Francis Tata and two other youths in our midst came up to me that they had a serious question they would want me to answer. I told them they had all the liberty to ask me any question and I assured them that to the best of my ability I was going to sincerely satisfy them. They were happy to hear my assuring words and readiness to satisfy them.

"Please Sir; we want to know if Ni John Fru Ndi has sent food to us here since our arrest and detention?" was their question.

I reflected and turned the matter up and down in my mind. To my mind this was not the type of serious question they raised my appetite for. Not knowing the angle from which they were coming, I quipped, "What is special about food from Ni? We are not starving. Look at the corner there filed with all kinds of fruits and foods. We have more than enough and we even feed others."

Seeing that I was trying to avoid the issue, they came up forcefully pinning me down.

"Please Sir; just tell us the simple truth. Remember you and Dr Luma worked so closely with him for many years," said their spokesman emphatically holding me to a very tight corner.

"Well you know he visited us when we were brought here. What's more, he drove to the Commercial Avenue and lived the experience of our brutal arrest. But as for food, I am not aware of any food or any other assistance from him," I said seeing that the obvious could not be hidden.

Most satisfied with my answer, they landed boldly leaving no doubt in my mind.

"Sir, if it were Francophone arrested and detained here would he not have mobilised all Bamenda to cook food and feed them? How can you and our National Chairman, Dr Luma, who is also the Vice National Chairman of the SDF be detained here and he sends no food? Is that normal? Is it correct?"

To be honest with you I was stunned to numbness. It sounded like a death sentence passed on a condemned criminal not an ordinary question seeking an answer. So I had no answer to give at all. They knew the truth and had passed their judgement even before approaching me, it seems.

I now understood that these young men who had been very active in the SDF right from its founding had been watching, observing and making their notes. I then concluded that they did not come to me because they did not know, they came for confirmation and to pronounce their judgment, loud and clear to me and why not, through me to others. The lesson is that leaders should not take even the uneducated followers for granted. Every one, male or female, young or old, has a say, has full rights and sense of judgement. Leaders must be responsible, sensitive, open minded, fair to all at all times. And in a political struggle, ignoring any among the down trodden, you do so at your own peril. True leadership, I mean leadership that serves the collective interest must be consistent both in word and action and must set high standards and live up to the set standards. Avoid being consistently inconsistent! Your credibility is not measured by what you say nor is it by the big things that you do but by the little things that you constantly do.

I then understood that they came as a delegation on behalf of the rest. I thanked them for their sincerity and frankness in expressing their mind. I equally encouraged them to feel free at all times and bring up anything of interest for our discussion and edification of the group as a whole.

Life in Bamenda Central Prison was a mixture of the good and bad, the ugly and the beautiful. There were some who had been there for more than ten, fifteen years and without hope of ever regaining their liberty since periodic Presidential clemency itself has no yard stick for fairness. These were resigned to fate. They lived lonely and most miserable lives even among the crowd. Whenever in a lively and cheerful conversation you made them feel at home and cherished and they managed to summon a smile, it was still miserable and sorrowful. In their eyes you see furry and bitterness beyond description. Even in here they lived in their own world of hopelessness and desperation.

The inmates would organise football competitions and even cultural dances. It is activities like this that take away the boredom of prison life. Generally, prison terribly lacks variety thus making life dull, meaningless and uneventful. Whenever there was the opportunity for cultural dances, the natives of Oku, Nso, and Kom will thrill everyone. A small dusty field in the centre of the built-in prison yard at such moments served as the stadium where all gathered for entertainment. This gave opportunity to mix and discuss with others. To encourage them, the SCNC donated a football which was received respectfully. They knew it was from the leaders of the Southern Cameroons, the Southern Cameroons many knew not but in hope and faith eagerly looked up to.

The prison inmates also had their internal government and a court with a judge. Since we were looked up to as special detainees, and lived apart, we were not part of this internal outfit.

While members of the government functioned even within the day, the court, like an evil society, sat only at night when doors are locked securely from outside by warders who having done their job well would disappear with the keys till next morning.

To me the court was a brutal court and frequently inflicted corporal punishment on those convicted. You would hear the unfortunate victim cry like an animal as corporal punishment is being administered by other inmates. Whoever the judge was he was in charge of jungle justice. Without doubt the Prison Authorities knew and tacitly approved of it if not such extreme barbarism could not have persisted. At night there are warders on guard. From the concept of discipline within the prison system as I experienced it, such corporal punishment to them was in order. Here law and order mean the subordination of the subjects to constituted authority without the right to question and be told why. He who exercises authority and influence is always right and must be obeyed. Obedience is not solicited based on conviction and reason, it is imposed from above. Here in prison truth comes from above and there is nothing as rights, freedom, and justice. The boss endowed with unquestionable authority is always right and must be honoured and respected. What is self-evident is authority; order comes from above and from below is slavish obedience and submission.

To expect people nurtured under a ruthless tyrannical regime such as exists in Bamenda Prison to show love, mercy and justice to those they have the luck to boss and oppress even for a minute is to expect the hen to grow teeth before eating corn or to drink water without taking up its head. This is against the law of nature. This explains the Bamenda Prison court system. I believe its emblem, if at all there was any, projected a whip, a sword, tears, and blood.

What I got from this is that evil is contagious and a totalitarian regime can never build a harmonious society in which there is love, fairness, mercy, passion for the defence of the common good. Here society is fragmented: there is the class of the governors who must enjoy all rights, honour and below this you have the ruled that must suffer and endure all indignities without complaining because there is no one to give them a listening ear. The dominant factor in such a society is chaos, impunity, anyone exploiting any given opportunity to lord it over others for self-interest and aggrandisement. Those in authority are the elect to be worshipped by those under them. Leaders belong apart and are never to serve. They are not accountable to those under them. Public interest which must be cherished, preserved and defended is not the common property of all within the system. What matters is the will and interest of the boss who is accountable to none. Here it is the reign of an evil genius in an evil kingdom.

With our growing positive influence, thanks to our good will and education, I approached some of the leaders and had dialogue with them. Through this I advised them against adding salt to an existing painful sore in the name of discipline. I told them imprisonment or being in Awaiting Trial (AT) for whatever reason was punishment too much already. They should be lenient, tolerant and correct their friends in love. As victims of a bad system which must be changed they should not exhibit wickedness and hatred among themselves. I told them by being wicked to their fellow Southern Cameroonians they were in league with the oppressor who has subjugated all Southern Cameroonians.

A most painful fact that I gathered was that more than 85% of the youths imprisoned or in AT were accused of theft and other minor offences. These were healthy and dynamic youths bubbling with energy to be put into meaningful productive purposes for the growth and development of the society. But here being wasted away. I am not in the least saying that thievery is not bad or is not a crime and as such should be condoned. I had the luck of interviewing many from Bui and Donga Mantung Counties (divisions) and recording their offences, theft of goats, hen, coffee, beans which they sold to manage their life constituted the crimes that brought them to this dungeon. This took up more than 90% of the victims. You must ask, what is responsible for this?

The answer is simple: the lack of gainful employment. Due to extreme poverty some of them had to drop out from primary school or college for the parents could not pay the fees. This is an area starved of any kind of industry to employ the ever growing army of unemployed youths. Some of these have acquired skills while some with reasonable level of education are anxious to live a productive life but without opportunities. With hard conditions, they fall into temptations. Is it not said that the devil finds work for idle hands? Such increase the overcrowding in the prison. The prison is neither an alternative nor does it provide a solution. If it does anything at all, it is an industry for waste of man power and dehumanisation of the victims. In this dungeon, not even the most disciplined person with a high IQ could have anything positive to learn and take home for good. It is worse when the bulk of this are the youths, the pride and future of the nation. These should be equipped with sound knowledge and skills for self-fulfilment for they are the future and pride of the nation. But here they are being wasted away in moral bankruptcy for they have no nation of theirs: they are a stateless people under barbaric alien rule.

7

Not the First of Its Kind

One thing that readily comes to my mind about my previous arbitrary arrests and detentions is the reaction of my daughter Ngwa'ani Kendeh Nfor in 1992. My detention has always affected her so badly. I prayed this time around that this prison detention of 2001 should not be one detention too much for her. She, like my family, has had to understand and accept, painfully though, that on becoming a crusader for the truth, freedom and justice for my people, prison cell automatically becomes my second bedroom, this without any comfort, safety and security of any kind.

On October 25, 1992, I granted an interview over the VOA on the state of affairs following the proclamation of the presidential election results in which Fru Ndi the victor was declared the vanquished. This interview was to be followed by another the following day. By the time the phone rang on October 26th, it was my intimate friend and colleague in arms Zama Kimbi Ndefru who answered to report that I had already been arrested by heavily armed troops who invaded an SDF Rally in Bamenda which I went to address following the heavily flawed elections. He concluded by mournfully announcing that my whereabouts was not known. It was thus from this interview the world learnt of my arrest and the inferno in Bamenda.

Ngwa'ani narrated with tearful eyes, their predicament that fateful day October 26th 1992. She said as gun firing and explosions of tear gas and grenades went on un-intermittently in the heart of Bamenda town, she and her four younger brothers clung together in their bed room without a father and a mother to comfort and assure them of their safety and security. Here stateless children became parentless. Double tragedy!

She told me the first time someone came in and inquired the whereabouts of their father; she took it for granted. But when a second and a third person ran in breathlessly and asked the same question and left in the same hasty and worried manner without a word, she had only one prayer: "Let it not be that our father has been killed and dumped in a gutter!" This worry was justifiable for since October 23rd when the results of the heavily flawed presidential elections were announced over radio from Yaoundé I had not been home with my family.

These concerned interrogators were SDF militants fleeing from the armed-invaded SDF rally organised to condemn the Yaoundé regime for staging an electoral coup and seizing Fru Ndi's victory. I was the lone member of the National Executive on hand who addressed the rally. The heavily-armed invading troops arrived when I was on the podium. Heavily militarised Bamenda town with burnt houses, deserted streets littered with all kinds of debris, the mortuary with the bulleted dead bodies, and many wounded on hospital beds in extreme agony, was like a recently captured town where you see more troops than civilians.

I listened to her with awe-inspiring concern after I left the gendarme cell Up Station that 1992. Firstly, I admired her courage. Secondly, I had pity for her, seeing that at her tender age she was convinced her father could so easily be barbarically murdered in cold blood for opposing an authoritarian regime. It is indeed sad to note that even babes, teenagers in annexed and occupied Southern Cameroons know how callous and diabolic the Yaoundé regime, as symbolised by the trigger-happy and repressive gendarme, is.

In a Pastoral Letter issued by the Archdiocese of Bamenda, 29th Nov. 1992, calling for earnest prayers for the abolition of torture and victims of torture and the torturers, it is stated, "The unspeakable crime of torture exists in our midst, and has taken on truly horrendous proportions in Bamenda as from the night of Tuesday, 27th October 1992". Substantiating its conclusion it quoted from the Report of the Mission of the National Human Rights Commission to Bamenda November 14-16 1992 which among other observations noted with dismay that:

> "The brutality of the forces of law and order, particularly during arrests, is very alarming. Many detainees are continuously being subjected to psychological and physical torture some of whom we saw in great pain, with swollen limbs and genitals, blisters and deep wounds and cracks on skulls."(pp. 4-5).

How I got released from the gendarmerie detention camp that year 1992 after weeks of detention, God alone can explain. My early arrest, without doubt, obviously saved me from being with Justice Nyo Wakai and others at the BMM Bamenda. Indeed my very good friend Dr Zama Kimbi Ndefru, who was on hand to report of my arrest on Oct. 26th to the VOA, was "free" only for a while. He was later arrested to join Justice Nyo Wakai at the BMM. At gun point they were later ferried to Nkondengui maximum political prison, Yaoundé, as if they were war captives. To taste of hell fire, devil-inspired barbarity, you only need to be detained in a gendarme cell in Southern Cameroons. No human being treats anything created by God, worse than what we witnessed in 1992 at the gendarmerie Up Station, Bamenda.

On arrival Up Station, both those who brought us up and those who were waiting for our arrival, started beating and kicking us mercilessly. I felt my whole body hot as if I had been stung by a million angry bees whose peace in their sanctuary I had turned upside down. At gun point we were made to squat down. Any hesitation was an invitation for the military boots or booth of the gun or belt on any choice part of your body, the head being the most favoured.

A gendarme standing at some point would mark out some unfortunate victim and scream, *"Lui la c'est le plus dangereux"* and land his heavy army shoes or gun booth on the victim's head. As you collapsed to the ground in awful pain, that gave them great amusement and laughter. To fail to wriggle in pain and cry for pity, mercy, to prove that you are tough and feel no pain is to invite the inferno on you at noon day in tropical Africa. And in the spirit of the brutes that they are, they will mercilessly give it to you. These torturers have no mercy. It was their entertainment and they enjoyed doing it in turns. It was not just competition but merciless torture to see who excels in bestiality.

After merciless torture that October 26, 1992, we were stripped naked; left only with pants. One after another, we were forced to pose for a picture, with your name boldly written on a cardboard and hanging on your neck, like an old rusty chain on a *"ngong"* dog. This was followed by interrogation by a squad of gendarmes ferried into Bamenda from la République. In satanic menacing arrogance they spoke only the 'holy' authoritative language, French.

The interrogation was humanly dehumanising and psychologically brutal and intimidating. It was part of the humiliating tactic adopted to cow you into slavish submission and prove to every Southern Cameroonian and in particular the "stubborn or head strong Bamenda man" that his life was in the hands of his lord from la République du Cameroun who could do and undo. In arrogant mocking language we were consistently reminded that "Bamenda as a whole could be wiped out and Cameroun would still live on: how much less of you an individual ant?" This just reminded us of what they, under the French, did in fighting the so-called UPC terrorism through which whole villages were put to the torch and erased from the face of the earth. But our country was not part of their French Cameroun. Treating us like a conquered people this historical and legal reality means nothing and does not appeal to them. A people who believe in brute force and that might is right do not entertain truth and legality. To them truth and legality are a luxury for theoreticians and classroom philosophers.

This was the hostile atmosphere we lived in the gendarmerie cell Up Station. For the period of incarceration you neither saw sun rise, sun set nor did you see who ever brought food to you. We were detained incommunicado.

At moments like this the gun-toting gendarme exhibits the limitlessness of his arrogance; wickedness and bestiality that can even make the devil on his throne in the lake of fire weep for the Southern Cameroonian. But these are a people brought up under a different culture of tolerance, respect for human dignity, the supremacy of the law, and a rich democratic culture brutally subjected to the inferno of tyranny.

When it was my turn to face the interrogation, or is it inquisition! I was ushered in. You move in with your nerves deadened as if you were going to your hang-man.

Immediately I stepped in the officer looked at my identity card in his hand menacingly and then at my face scornfully. Then he asked officiously in the commanding language, French, "*Est-ce-que vous êtes celui qu'on appelle* Nfor Nfor?" (i.e., "Are you the one called Nfor Nfor?"). I answered, "Yes". As if not convinced, he asked the second and third time, each time viciously scrutinising both the identity card and my face. Receiving the same answer and convinced that the half nude person before him was the stone-head man called Nfor Nfor, he said "*votre cas est special*" (i.e. For you, your case is special). I sat stiff and motionless. Was it my spirit and will or the physical person? Or was it the two combined? It is hard to say. But we have every reason to thank God there was a chair for me to sit on. Had I been made to stand, my limbs would not have borne the burden the half trunk up carried.

That ended the inquisition and I was told to go out. I was pushed with the booth of the gun to join some forty four others in a squalid cell with a bucket at the right hand corner for a toilet. Stinking dirty water was draining in from one other room. You had no choice and facing you mockingly was "NO HOPE!"

Scores were on the floor in agonising pain nursing their wounds with tears while their captors were feeling good outside and scornfully mocking as a tortured captive is pushed in and unable to walk saunters and collapses on others lifelessly. We were treated worse than war captives.

As in 1992 when the agent of the tyrannical regime could not believe that the person before him was Nfor Nfor, and had to ask three times; in 2001 each delegation that came in from Yaoundé to scold and intimidate us, never finished its mission without someone from the group asking, "who is Nfor Nfor?" or "where is the person called Nfor Nfor?" This only gave an opportunity for them to leave with a firm message on what we stand for from me and others who cared to speak out, such as Pa Stephen Ndi and the National Chairman, Dr Martin Ngeka Luma. Our firmness and courage in telling them what we stand for and where the struggle will lead us to namely, the restoration of the statehood of British Southern Cameroons; was always too much for them to bear. On their last visit after addressing them, I handed to Dr Solomon Nfor Gwei, the Chairman of la République's toothless Human Rights Commission, and the usual lame leader of the team a copy of the "56 Theses..." (Chapter Eleven). Some other members of the delegation took copies and I challenged them to prove me wrong on the facts contained therein. This was the third and last delegation visit from Yaoundé we had.

It is significant that a statement or two be made on this fateful day October 26, 1992 in the light of my family and my commitment to the fight for freedom, justice, democracy and independence for our people.

On this fateful day my wife, Mary Nan Nfor, was battling with her sister-in-law, Mrs Priscilia Ngum, begging the francophone proconsuls, Senior Divisional Officer for Mezam, Sufo Samuel, and North West Governor, Bel Luc Rene, alas, "Grenade" in mournful memory of those murdered by grenades and the grenade amputees, to be merciful to them and grant them passage to convey the remains of Gideon Ngum, the Divisional Officer of Muyuka, Fako County (Division) to his native village in Oku for burial. Gideon Ngum was murdered in the presence of his children by a mob on the 23rd October 1992 when the presidential election results were announced. To every Southern Cameroonian it was the most barbaric murder, a thing never

ever imagined. The children screamed, wailed, groaned in horrific pain and watched helplessly as no policeman or gendarme made any effort to save their beloved father and boss of the security in the area. Like many other criminal and brutal things that took place within that most horrific period, no investigation was ever conducted into the brutal murder of this fine gentleman.

But how came it that the representative of the President in the administrative area was murdered on the day the boss, Mr President Paul Biya, won his elections? Hard to say, you may conclude. But in keeping with the rigidly Napoleonic centralised system imposed in British Southern Cameroons, as the Divisional Officer for Muyuka, it was his primary duty to defend the interest of his boss in his area of jurisdiction. We however recall that Gideon Ngum was of the North West Province, the home province of Fru Ndi who challenged incumbent President Paul Biya and he, Fru Ndi, is said to have won the elections. It should also be recalled that when Fru Ndi could not file his registration papers, as the hour was closing on, it was Gideon Ngum in Muyuka who accepted and registered the candidature of Ni John Fru Ndi. Let it be understood that he, Gideon Ngum, violated no law, he only complied with the law and he did it within his competence. Had he violated the law, Fru Ndi's candidature should have been nullified.

But why did he (Gideon Ngum) have to die such a painful death? The life of citizens of an occupied territory hangs in the balance; even corps enjoys no better treatment. The subjugated of an occupied territory do not have and enjoy the right to life according to God's will; they exist at the mercy of their oppressors and captors.

This explains why despite the pleadings, the coffin bearing Gideon Ngum could not traverse Bamenda where he had lived and worked for years. In defence of the imposed state of emergency, my wife and the sister-in-law, Mrs Priscilia Ngum, had to be issued a *"laissez passer"* each to enable them move out of Bamenda, since the corps could not enter Bamenda. They had to move to Bafoussam to meet the corps and from there to Fombort all in West Province, la République du Cameroun territory, before arriving Bui, then to Oku. This made the journey more than five times longer.

This aside, the psychological torture, the harassment, provocation, intimidation they suffered in the hands of the occupation forces at the countless check points from Nkwen to Up Station to meet the colonial authorities, my wife says, there is no language to describe. Though all of North West was under a state of emergency and Fru Ndi, the supposed winner of the elections, under house arrests, Bamenda town was under a military siege. Torture, rape, looting, maiming, and extra-judicial executions in gendarme cells were as normal as sunrise in tropical Africa. The inhabitants were as helpless as a life fish dumped on a rock in the Sahara Desert at noon day.

In the new Southern Cameroons human liberty and the dignity of man shall be central to the principle of good governance and special attention and special programmes must be adopted for the transformation of the current barbaric prison system. Though I hold that Cameroon is a huge prison and every Southern Cameroonian, even the unborn in the mother's womb, is a prisoner, the truth is that the prison, as I saw it under la République du Cameroun occupation, is a system for the dehumanisation of the dehumanised Southern Cameroonian.

We who have dedicated our lives to the struggle for the RESTORATION of the Statehood and INDEPENDENCE of Southern Cameroons fervently believe that TRUTH is sacred for it is of God. TRUTH is eternal and there is no flood, no tornado and no volcanic eruption that can bury the TRUTH. TRUTH does not get consumed by fire. It does not decay. We equally believe that annexation is a crime against humanity and it must be fought and destroyed. If others have fought triumphantly: why not Southern Cameroonians!

I equally fervently hold that without respect and defence of truth there can never be social justice in society. The defence of truth goes with the promotion of human equality, human dignity and justice in society. A great preacher of the word, Fr. Tatah H. Mbuy, holds that, "Justice and truth are Siamese twins." (p. 19).

Fr. Tatah H. Mbuy in what I term his political epistle titled "Africa's New Experience in Multi-Party Democracy" (A Modern Challenge for the Local Church), observes:

> "For centuries, traditional and modern Africa lived and practised either a one-party democracy as in traditional setting or else she suffered under depressing and monolithic autocracies occasionally spiced with the ruthless rule of uniformed men. Hence whichever way one looked at the African people, they...groaned under the yoke of nauseating dictators." And he concludes, "The human being can only take so much for so long and like the L' HOMME REVOLTE of Albert Camua, he screams: "enough is enough." Such rebellion cannot be seen as subversion. On the contrary it reveals the deep human desire for the basic right of freedom. What we are witnessing in most modern Africa today can be rightly

termed a "second liberation" after the fall of colonialism." (p.4).

He who sleeps on his rights loses them but he who defends his rights lives in FREEDOM and DIGNITY. Will we, like South Africans, Namibians, and East Timorese in solidarity make or must we in treachery mar? What legacy are we leaving to the next generation? The greatest task of any age is to correct its own errors and fill its created pot holes in order to bequeath a rich legacy to the next generation. We of this generation are challenged to rededicate ourselves to being the beacon of good hope for the next generation of Southern Cameroonians and humanity in general.

Let it be pointed out to those who doubt our right to restore the statehood and independence of the Southern Cameroons that what we stand for is legitimate, is just, and is in conformity with international law and above all, the divine law. And as truth has never been defeated by falsehood, the good Lord of Justice will lead us triumphantly to victory. Our greatest enemy is fear, which we must, individually and collectively, subdue and bury. Fear is man's greatest enemy. As the lack of faith in Christ the saviour leads you to hell in the hereafter, submission to fear subjects you to perpetual servitude here on earth. Man under the influence of fear becomes a shadow of his natural self for he has denied himself his divine birth right and a place of honour and dignity here on earth and in history. Let no one fool you that submission to slavery and servitude in contradiction of your divine rights as a human being created in God's image is humility. This is treachery and a betrayal of God's will for you as a human being, born free and equal.

The international boundaries of Southern Cameroons were defined by treaty and demarcated at the same time as those of French Cameroun that adopted the name la République du Cameroun at independence. The two distinct territories were carved out of German Kamerun in March 1916, none being superior to the other. With the demise of the co-habitation or non-implementation of the federal union envisioned by the UN, restoration of self-sovereign existence becomes a natural right of each component state. We, as patriots, of the Fatherland, are legitimately fighting to restore the ancient landmark or international boundary, which la République du Cameroun on its agenda of aggression and expansionism has declared non-existent. To us, it is a historic duty; a task that must be done. This generation should write its name in the sands of history by righting the wrongs of 1961 in order to bequeath a befitting legacy to the future generation.

To consciously take a seat in the sanctuary of comfort and complacency while our people groan every day under the burdensome yoke of brutish oppression, annexation, colonial occupation, assimilation and the plunder of the wealth of the land is not only scandalous of the intellectuals and the Church of our time, it is out right treachery. I consistently challenged the men of God in their holy robes each time they visited us in prison to tell me "What will be left of the Bible if these three words, Truth, Love, and Justice were removed from the holy book!" Do these three words not constitute the holy names of the Lord of all creation? In Eastern Europe and in apartheid South Africa, the Church played a significant role in sensitising and educating the masses to fight against gross injustice, the subjugation of God's people to misery and untimely death. This gave birth to what came to be popularly known as "liberation theology". But why is the situation in British Southern Cameroons different? People in society, who by their respectable position are expected to speak out, seem to be watching and fearing their shadows. This seems to explain why Dr Bernard Fonlon, a great son of this land, British Southern Cameroons, cried out loud for the birth of the "Genuine Intellectual," the change agent, the transformer from the bad to the good.

An intellectual should not be known by his academic titles nor should he use such to cow down the wretched of the earth in his society. An intellectual known by his titles is a pseudo-intellectual. A real intellectual or the genuine intellectual should be endowed with a heart and conscience for a better humanity, should be known by his capacity to inspire and move his people from ignorance to knowledge, from poverty to prosperity and from servitude and subjugation to freedom and dignity. To an intellectual truth is infinite and must be defended at all cost. An intellectual worthy of his name must be humble, a true servant of the people, a change-agent; he must hate evil, injustice and must be a crusader for human freedom and justice and guarantor for better humanity.

It is said that many will die without the opportunity to read the bible let alone hear the gospel and be converted. But what you do and your character constitutes a whole revelation of who you are and your true place in history. Many who come across you, those who live and share with you will read you like a book and draw their conclusion. By your character, which is read every day, some who may never read the redemptive message of Christ in the bible will either be led to the waiting arms of the Saviour for eternal life or to the devil for eternal damnation. The cry of the orphans and widows, victims of gross injustice, the amputees and the many who have deliberately and grossly been denied a future rise up to the high heavens and the Lord is most concerned about the stand of the Church and your personal responds. How will the people know the truth which should set them free when you team up with the oppressors of the vulnerable, when you refuse to speak out against injustice? Silence in the face of gross injustice is treacherous.

I believe it was on the full understanding of the gravity of this evil act that led this great man of God and crusader for human freedom, justice, human equality and human dignity, Dr Martin Luther King Jr. to declare this eternal truth of all ages and cultures. He said, "The ultimate tragedy is not the oppression and cruelty by the bad people but the silence over that by the good people."

Is the Church in Southern Cameroons the salt of the land? Is it playing the transforming and purifying role? Is it warning the leaders of their crimes and sin against the widows, orphans and the vulnerable of the society or it is compromising and condoning? Is it playing the role of light exposing the ills perpetuated by the holy cows of the society or it is playing safe and covering-up? It is not enough to sit in the sanctuary of the church or Cathedral praying that there be justice in society without speaking out or lifting a finger! Change according to God's standard came to Nineveh only when Jonah spoke out and lashed out at the oppressors and exploiters and those violating God's law.

Once at the World Council of Churches Headquarters, in Geneva, the authorities listened to me with rapt attention and where shocked to hear what I narrated to them as the fate of our people. At the end one of them asked me, "What has been the role of the Church?" I sincerely told them that some few pastors have suffered arrests and detentions for praying or preaching and mentioning the SCNC or for being caught with SCNC literature. This sounded as not enough.

> "We have met many Church authorities from your country at our conferences," one disturbed authority confessed, "but they have never raised such a grave situation of gross injustice targeted against a particular part of the country and people".

Must the Church in British Southern Cameroons make or mar? Can it afford to be indifferent and silent in the face of gross injustice and human degradation? If so in whose interest or at whose detriment! Fr. Tatah H. Mbuy holds that as much as Clerics should not indulge in partisan politics and hold posts,

> "...the church cannot remain silent in the face of abuses and crime against humanity from wherever and whoever they come. If she were to be silent in this matter, this would be a flagrant and sacrilegious betrayal of her mission on earth."(p. 9).

This is what the Master and Head of the Church, who firmly took sides with the poor, the down trodden and the oppressed, defines as the ordained mission of the Church and whoever claims to stand and speak for Him and in His name must understand, believe fervently and practice. Christ the Lord said:

> "The spirit of the Lord God is upon me; because the Lord hath anointed me to preach good tidings unto the

meek; he hath sent me to bind up the broken-hearted, to proclaim liberty to the captives, and the opening of the prison to them that are bound." Isaiah 61:1 (King James Version).

From the holy book we are further told that the people perish for lack of vision and that they live in perpetual anguish when the wicked rule. Where can people live in perpetual anguish more than in a country under annexation, colonial occupation, foreign domination, alien rule, assimilation and naked exploitation of the people's God-given wealth? In which type of society do you have more people in urgent need of liberty, more people in prison to be set free and hungrier for the message of good hope and good tidings than in a nation under foreign domination and alien rule? Should the Church not stand as a light house helping politicians, the pseudo-intellectuals, the economic elite, the traditional authorities and other managers of the commonweal, to cultivate critical thought, nurture a dynamic culture of dialogue and reconciliation? Should the Church not inspire those who have teamed up with the oppressor and exploiter against the people or the absolute majority, to love and defend truth, human freedom, equality, dignity and uphold justice as the foundation of enduring peace and progress in society? Should the Church not be the true Town Crier consistently and systematically vehemently denouncing the injustices inflicted on the down trodden and the naked policies of divide and rule for self-perpetuation in power?

We must not forget that the empire and colonial builders of yesterday used the bible and the sword together for the grandeur and prestige of their imperial nations at the detriment of the African and third world in general. If that was the role of some of the early missionaries the reverse today must be the case for the truth we have come to know must set us free. The church today must be a change agent, indeed a liberator for the Creator in his infinite wisdom created all men free and equal.

While in Eastern Europe and South Africa, for example, the Church provided sanctuary to the oppressed and openly fought for the right to self-determination, human freedom, human equality, democracy, but here in British Southern Cameroons the Church has tended to bow to the dictates of the Yaoundé dictatorship and barred the SCNC from even using Church premises as before. The SCNC was born at the Catholic Maternity Home, Buea in 1993, and in 1994 the Bamenda Proclamation was adopted at the Presbyterian Church, Ntabesi, Nkwen. In the early days of the struggle, some Church authorities held positions in the movement and played active roles. All those who served as Chaplains of the struggle have since withdrawn. Have they been intimidated by Yaoundé through the top leaders of the denominations? Is the annexationist dictator in Yaoundé doing God's will and defending the TRUTH by declaring that Cameroun, which includes British Southern Cameroons, is one and indivisible? Can fraud and illegality be transformed into legality by the passage of time? Where is JUSTICE and Fairness when a child who passed in Religious Knowledge at the GCE Advance Level is disqualified for admission into university or recruitment into the police force or army, and employment because this subject is not recognised by government? How does the same government recognise it as a GCE subject but not recognise same as relevant qualification for employment and higher studies?

What accounts for the closure of all sea, river and air ports in Southern Cameroons and concentration of all maritime trade and air transportation in Douala, la République du Cameroun? What justifies the closure of viable economic and financial institutions set up by the defunct Southern Cameroons Government such as the Ntem Oil Palm Plantation, the Santa Coffee Estate, the Yoke Electricity station, the Development Agency for the establishment and improvement of small and medium size enterprises? What was responsible for the transfer of Southern Cameroons Bank, and the National Produce Marketing Board, (NPMB) headquarters to Yaoundé and Douala respectively, la République territory, and the confiscation of the farmers' huge stabilisation fund saved for the rainy day by the Yaoundé authorities who had no part in the savings?

Why is royalty for oil paid to Douala City Council, la République du Cameroun, and not to Victoria Council or Ndian Councils, Southern Cameroons, from where the black gold is extracted? Is it not incredible and indeed paradoxical that Ndian from where the black gold is exploited does not have even a petrol station, an inch of tarred road, is most under developed and that petrol is more expensive in the land of its extraction, Southern Cameroons, than in la République du Cameroun? Is Yaoundé challenging God's infinite wisdom in locating the black gold in Southern Cameroons soil and not in la République du Cameroun soil? Can there be love, harmony, enduring peace where truth is not respected and there is no justice? Why is a Southern Cameroonian unfit to be Minister of Foreign Affairs, Defence, Territorial Administration, Finance, Education, National Security, Secretary General at the Presidency, let alone President of the country? Does this not beyond pardon prove that there are two distinct Cameroons and one, la République du Cameroun, has illegally annexed and occupied the other, namely, British Southern Cameroons and is treating the latter as a conquered territory and its citizens as their under dogs and the wretched of the earth? The rays of the sun do not cease to shine on the truth because the tyrant has distorted the history of the subjugated.

To rise up and vehemently and uncompromisingly challenge the evil status quo as Arch Bishop Desmond Tutu did in South Africa is to defend the divine will of the Creator and to live for humanity. Man lives not in days but in deeds. He was created to live in the service of his fellow man for the glory of his Lord. Life worthy of its divine purpose is shared life; life lived in service not in solitary comfort. Service to society or nation contributes to human progress and world democracy and peace based on justice. Before a people's victory is written in books, it is written by the visionary patriots that inspire the masses to courageous positive action for freedom and dignity according to divine will. God in his infinite wisdom did not create free men, on the one hand, and slaves on the other. All men were created free, equal and given the right to dominate the world but never to be dominated by others. And none of us is here by his making or design, by chance or accident. It is by the infinite will of the Creator who sent each of us here on mission to suffer no man and wrong none for the glory of Him who sent each of us. But that each should honour and live by the golden rule of "Do unto others as you would want them do unto you".

And speaking realistically: is the SCNC violating any written law or natural principle in its Non-violent struggle for freedom and justice for British Southern Cameroonians? Is the SCNC telling a lie that British Southern Cameroons is not an integral part of la République du Cameroun and that there is no legal union between the two distinct peoples and nations? Even if there was a legal union, under international law has la République du Cameroun any superior right to confiscate the inherent and unquestionable right of Southern Cameroons to restore its distinct identity if not satisfied with the union?

Did SCNC leaders and followers abuse the sovereign rights of la République du Cameroun by commemorating the independence of Southern Cameroons on their own land? Did they commit any crime to warrant extra-judicial execution, maiming, arrest, and torture and prison detention? By commemorating Southern Cameroons' independence anniversary on Southern Cameroons soil, in what way, whichever, did they disturb the peace of the people and government of la République du Cameroun? Reflect deeply, please meditate, and speak out truthfully for freedom and justice sake!

But forget not that on January 01, 1990 la République du Cameroun under President Paul Biya celebrated the 30th anniversary of their independence. To immortalise the historic significance of this event a postage stamp worth 1000Francs CFA was issued with the map of their country, la République du Cameroun conspicuously displayed. It is instructive to note that this map does not include British Southern Cameroons for it was not an integral part of French Cameroun when it acceded to independence on January 01, 1960. And under international law British Southern Cameroons has never been and is today not an integral part of la République du Cameroun.

In the celebration of their 30ᵗʰ anniversary of independence they did not involve us and we did not disturb their right to their peaceful and quiet celebration. Why did Mr Biya decide to use his repressive forces in 2001 to make our peaceful commemoration bloody?

The position adopted by SCNC leaders and activists is inspired by love and defence of truth, fatherland, international law and conventions, pride and consciousness of identity and faith in their determination underpinned by the UN Charter and international instruments. The purpose is to restore their statehood and be masters of their destiny. In this they have an eternal lesson from Moses of the bible as recorded in Hebrews 11: 24-29. Here we are told Moses when he was grown up discovered that he was a Jew and not a prince of Egypt. Consequently, he chose to identify and suffer with his enslaved brothers and sisters instead of living in unjustified legendary affluence with the hope of becoming the next King Pharaoh in a foreign country over the blood of his enslaved people. Moses was a faithful servant of God, a nationalist, a Jewish patriot and a freedom fighter and crusader for justice for his people. He believed in the supremacy of the living Lord, the creator of the visible and invisible. He was not ashamed of his roots. On the contrary, he was proud of his identity and under existing circumstances firmly defended same. As one who feared and worshipped God his Creator, he was equally a believer in human equality, dignity and firm defender of the fact that God created all men equal and to each people the Creator ordained their inheritance which they must cherish and defend.

God by creating all human beings free and equal, ordained that no one should be a slave of another and no people should be dominated by another. Moses saw the contradiction and gave his life to be a change agent. And God by choosing Moses, a Jew to lead the Israelites out of bondage established the eternal rule that each people must be ruled by someone from among them and never a foreigner. Here God has not only declared foreign domination and alien rule as evil, those who collaborate, and those who surrender to are as guilty of this evil as those who impose it.

Moses proved beyond any reasonable doubt that he was a man with a heart for others; one who cares, one who is concerned about the welfare, wellbeing and happiness of his people. A man with a heart for others, not just about self, but one who seeks to know and defend the truth. He stood for the truth, equality and justice. And caring and knowing the truth leads to positive action that brings about necessary change, human transformation that lifts the down trodden and the subjugated to know, defend and enjoy their self-worth.

If God inspired and empowered him to be the transforming and efficient leader that he turned out to be, it was his faith and willingness to descend into the abyss of dehumanisation, servitude and oppression with his kindred. In the abyss of servitude with his people he better understood the gravity of servitude which violates natural justice, the rhythm of nature's beauty and the divine purpose for man and from this pit of human degradation God raised him and equipped him to lead the Jews from bondage to freedom in their own land. It was his readiness to humble himself, lead a transforming life and serve his people by living a shared life rather than live for self. This made him a great leader.

Queen Esther, in Esther chapter 4 like Moses, demonstrates exceptional qualities of care and deep concern for her people. The vain trappings of office, affluence, grandeur, prestige did not blind her to forget her roots, her natural identity according to God's infinite wisdom. Because she cared and was ready even to die to save her people she prayed, she fasted and took the risk of defiling the law at the risk of her life just to speak out to the king in defence of her people. Because she stood for the truth in defence of her people, she did not die and all her people were saved.

I also fervently believe that had Nelson Mandela thought more of himself, his comfort, safety, security and high prospects of him becoming a respectable lawyer in apartheid South Africa, had he for self-aggrandisement collaborated with the apartheid regime, this evil system would have been flourishing in South Africa even today. Who knows if with Ian Smith and his Unilateral Declaration of Independence, (UDI) in Southern Rhodesia, (Zimbabwe), this evil regime would not have spread to the rest of the southern region of Africa? By committing himself to living a shared life: indeed a life of humility and service, Nelson Mandela has not only brought freedom and genuine democracy to his native land South Africa; he has become a legend in his own life time and made the black race proud and great the world over.

Until you give God first place in your life you can never understand and appreciate the divine purpose and predetermined mission for your being here on earth. But you surrender your life to the devil for his evil purposes; you will become a vicious instrument of human suffering and degradation. While God empowers you for human goodness and blesses you abundantly for fulfilling the purpose for which he created you, the devil uses you and demands a heavy price which sometimes takes your own life if you do not faithfully comply with the devil's conditions or demands. You just need to listen to the awful ordeals of those who deal with occult powers. The devil demands from you only that which you cherish most. By serving self and the devil you become a curse for your people.

Each of us is endowed with great talents but until they are put to work for a better humanity, until you positively become sensitive to human condition and commit yourself to being an agent of transformation, the endowed talents in you will never bloom and blossom. Are you an agent of change, positive change? Are you the shining star of positive change in the abyss of darkness and desolation? Are you a source of hope and comfort for the broken-hearted?

8

A Taste of Hell by Extension

What existed and confronted us in the Bamenda Central Prison was a microcosm of what takes place in the larger society. Bamenda like the larger Southern Cameroons society was brought under this reign of terror as a consequence of the 1961 treachery. Thus Southern Cameroonians who had grown under a system in which a police man was a friend not a foe of the ordinary citizen and was never armed with life bullets; without any transitional period to adjust, suddenly on mid night of October 1st 1961 came under gendarmes armed to the teeth with mortal bullets. They spoke a foreign language, French, and their manner of behaviour was/is authoritarian. The Pastoral Letter of the Archdiocese of Bamenda has this to say of British Southern Cameroons:

> "Torture, cruel, inhuman and degrading treatment was totally unheard of in the Cameroons under United Kingdom Trusteeship. It was inconceivable in the British Cameroons for a policeman to slap anyone, let alone torture him. Let us pray that the priceless heritage of respect for the human person which prevailed in the British Cameroons may soon be recovered and shared among the people…" (p. 7).

The reign of terror and gendarme heavy handedness which many a Southern Cameroonian before October 1st 1961 treated as fairy tale or took for granted as a thing of distant land and some could not imagine how human beings survived under, was no longer imaginary: it had long become the hot air of hell they breath every blessed day of their life here on earth. The first incidence of the reign of terror on Southern Cameroons soil with grave consequences was the Tombel massacre.

While in Nkambe, headquarters of the then Nkambe Division (Donga Mantung County) inhabitants woke up one early April 1962 morning subjected to gendarme invasion and serious beatings with military belts, truncheons and gun booths, in Tombel, then Kumba Division (Meme County) such show of military force was far on a larger scale resulting in many deaths. From Tombel many were as well arrested and kidnapped for detention in Yaoundé. Many carried to Yaoundé never saw Tombel, the land of their ancestors again.

The unprovoked brutal attacks in Nkambe and Tombel, of the former Kumba Division, were without doubt premeditated. These two divisions out of the then six administrative divisions of British Southern Cameroons constituted the bastion of the opposition to union with la République du Cameroun. And in the plebiscite, having been deprived of outright sovereign independence, they voted heavily for what they knew better, namely, federation with Nigeria.

Human life and human blood which to many was sacred, was to become a thing of the past as the state of emergency under which French Cameroun came to be ruled as from 1955 was extended to Southern Cameroons. Tombel's proximity to the territory infested with the terrorist hide out provided a good excuse for gendarmes and police to practically demonstrate what it takes to live under the new order and the innocent paid for dearly. Since then many other Southern Cameroons towns have come under this baptism of fire, the fire which Fon Achirimbi of Bafut in Mamfe, 1959 said French Cameroun represents "FIRE" and called on his fellow compatriots to fight for their separate sovereign independence.

Under President Ahidjo's reign torture and systematic repression was the instrument of state policy. The decrees and laws that protected this system of state policy made it appear as if without, the state would cease to be or the absence of will make the state irrelevant. Here the state was understood in the context of the leader who rules and reigns absolutely and his continuous in power. The Ahidjo decree No. 62/OF/18 of 12 March 1962 (on the repression of subversive activities), states:

> Art. 1. "Any person who in any manner whatsoever incites any other person to resist in any manner whatsoever the application of the laws, decrees, regulations or orders of any public administrative authority shall be guilty of a misdemeanour and shall be liable to a fine of 100,000 to 1 million francs or to imprisonment for a period from 3 months to 3 years or to both such fine and imprisonment.
> Art. 2. "Any person who acts in any manner likely to bring to contempt or ridicule any public authority or who incites hatred against the Government of the Federal Republic or any federated state or who takes part in any subversive enterprise against the authorities or the laws of the said Republic or Federated States or who aids and abets any such enterprise shall be guilty of a misdemeanour and shall be liable to a fine of 200,000 to 2 million francs or to imprisonment for a period from 1 to 5 years or to both such fine and imprisonment".

Against freedom of the press, expression and opinion, Art. 3, states, "Any person who publishes or reproduces any false statement, rumour or report or any tendentious comment on any statement or report which is likely to bring into hatred, contempt or ridicule any public authority shall be guilty of a misdemeanour and shall be liable to the penalties provided in Article 2 of this ordinance."

However before independence two acts were enacted in 1959 for the purpose of safe guarding 'public order', namely, the state of *'mise en guarde'* and the 'state of alert'. With independence in 1960 this was re-enforced with Presidential Decree No.52 of 7 May, 1960 which became the 'organic law of the state of emergency.'

With this legal backing torture became a state controlled machinery to suppress dissent no matter how legitimate. With this suspects and victims are subjected to the most flagrant abuses such as solitary confinement known only by the captors, humiliation even in public before family members and friends, flogging, psychological pressure and physical pain and other barbaric means used to extract information, force victim to confess and reveal other associates who will equally be arrested and tortured, physical elimination and disappearances.

The word subversion, which came into "popular" usage, could imply many things- the use of words, asking a question to instead of praising the authority, or any action unacceptable to the authority before you. A young man could be a victim for clashing with a "big man" over a beautiful girl friend. Labelling such as subversive was never subjected to any court of law but as determined by the authority. His judgement was final and the victim had no means to seek redress. Such flagrant abuse of human rights became the order of the day. The gendarme was ubiquitous and seen as a symbol of terror by the common man. The mere appearance of a gendarme in a market place or village, in the early days of the so-called federation could have men, women and children fleeing as if a wild tornado had swept through or as if the court yard has been invaded by a lion. A gendarme, simply put, was not seen and accepted as a normal human being in British Southern Cameroons.

President Ahidjo wasted no time following the creation of the fake federation in issuing the Federal Ordinance 61/OF/4 of October 4, 1961 setting up a number of Military Courts in Southern Cameroons which were to handle all matters of the slightest political nature and to empower them to expeditiously administer swift and exceptional rigorous repression against the enemies of the state which he embodied.

It needs be pointed out that while the judgement of a military court may not be appealed against to the Supreme Court, the Minister of Justice with the consent of the Minister of the Armed Forces may order a retrial by another military court if not satisfied with the first judgement.

In the pursuit of its repressive agenda, notorious governmental agencies charged with 'intelligence' gathering, spying and torture were set up to perfect the system. In 1959 the *'service de documentation'* (SEDOC) was created. This was the Cameroun brand of the French *'service de documentation exterieure et de contre espionage'* (SDECE) modelled after the French system by two French SDECE experts seconded to Ahidjo for that purpose. Next to be created was the *Brigades Mixtes Mobiles* (BMM). BMM centres usually have special rooms underground, christened *'Chapele'* or *'where God does not exist.'* In here sadists subject their victims to bestial torture and degrading punishment. Techniques of torture similar to what obtained in apartheid South Africa and imperialist wars, for example, against the Algerian nationalists include the *bastanade*, various practices of asphyxiation, electric shocks, the old *falanga* method i.e. beating on the soles of feet, the *balançoire*, hanging, disappearances, and outright murder, among others.

By seconding experts to establish the secret political police system in Cameroun Paris was acting in conformity with the Cooperation Accords, namely, *Pacte Coloniale*, signed with Ahidjo on November 13, 1959. This umbilical cord relationship between SEDOC and SDECE with Paris pulling the strings and dictating the tune under Foccart whose mission was to facilitate the elimination of enemies of France's favoured regimes was to pave the way for the flourishing of French neo-colonialism in Africa and in this regard, Cameroun was strategic to the necessary success in the Central African sub region.

The mapping of cooperation ties between the local secret security system and French secret services took place against the back drop of the UPC rebellion, a nationalist movement forced into rebellion by the autocratic French colonial rule. Already since 1955 there were French forces on Cameroun soil deeply involved in counter insurrectionist struggle. Serving neo-colonial interest and with defence constituting an important pillar of the Cooperation Agreement the detachment of these forces were to be stationed in the territory for a long time even after independence. The UPC rebellion simply only provided a good excuse for France to establish its hegemonic dominance and draw Cameroun into neo-colonial embrace. Cameroun's Ahidjo was a willing partner, no, a tool for through French military intervention the UPC rebellion was brutally suppressed and he survived in power and was determined to retain for a long time to come.

By the 1970 Cameroun had the largest military establishment in French-speaking Africa. Consuming about a fifth (19.6%) of the national budget, it received the highest allocation at the detriment of services such as education, health, infrastructural development and agriculture which were necessary for development of the human potential and sound economic take-off.

In maintaining the established umbilical cord relationship between Paris and Yaoundé there were always French military personnel posted as special advisers to various units of the military while other experts were sent to the Presidency as Advisers to the President on Military and Security Affairs. Does this alone not make the idea of the so-called Federal Republic of Cameroon not being member of the Francophone bloc or the Commonwealth meaningless political slogan to deceive the subjugated Southern Cameroonian? How many of these expert advisers were British? Did Britain ever send military experts as advisers to the Cameroun Presidency or Army?

Ahidjo and his advisers did not in the least lose sight of the fact that British Southern Cameroons, if a genuine federal system were allowed, would be coming in with a more appealing political philosophy, governmental system and rule of law that defends and promotes human equality, dignity, and peace based on justice. To maintain the status quo and serve French neo-colonial interest, on which his survival in power depended, Ahidjo reneged on his 1959 pronouncement at the UNGA to respect Southern

Cameroons distinct identity and never to annex the territory. He saw equal partnership in the building of the Federation made up of two states equal in status as a threat to his survival in power, a violation of *Pacte Coloniale*, which is the cooperation agreement meant to protect and promote French interest of which he (Ahidjo) was the local CEO.

As per the Paris/Yaoundé hidden agenda the so-called unification was not the building of a new Cameroon to mirror the legitimate aspirations of the citizens of the two distinct nation states; it was the expansion of French interest in West Africa through annexation and assimilation of a former British trust territory. Federation was a mere comforting deception to draw British Southern Cameroons into full embrace for annexation. Ahidjo being a hard core Gaullist was a good student of Gaullist dictum of "la federation c'est la secession" and right from the beginning, thanks to available French political and constitutional experts, he put in place institutions for a rigid centralized state. Consequently, the Anglo-Saxon system had to be attacked with full force through the imposition of a new political culture and assimilation through the use of instruments of coercion, patronage and unbridled corruption.

As Southern Cameroons swiftly came under the state of emergency that had been reigning in la République, BMM centres were created in Kumba, bordering the Mungo *Departement* and Bamenda bordering the Bamilike region, the heartbeat of the UPC rebellion. This was the price Southern Cameroons paid for surrendering to "independence by joining" as the UN failed to implement Resolution 1608 of April 21, 1961 thus facilitating annexation and colonial occupation by la République du Cameroun. This was viciously implemented as the UK and UN turned their backs looking the other way while Yaoundé, in the interest of Paris, did as deemed necessary.

Thus the hopes of a loose federal union within which Southern Cameroonians were going to live their life according to their cherished core values of freedom of movement, assembly, expression, and of thought without French ways of life and heavy handedness of the dreaded gendarme, as the KNDP preached during the plebiscite campaigns, was shattered with promptitude. Yaoundé did not want to be contaminated with the liberal democratic culture flourishing in Southern Cameroons and spared no second in imposing the new order. And there was no better way of doing it than the physical presence of the dreaded gendarme-(men in arms) which patriotic Southern Cameroonians cried out against as an "army of occupation".

French Cameroun was no open free society. It was a pure police state that had been governed by a totalitarian colonial regime. A totalitarian regime builds multiple security networks whose primary role is to spy, to repress and eliminate. Ahidjo serving as a faithful CEO of an outpost of French neo-colonial interest inherited all this hook, line, and sinker. To officers of this torture outfit unquestionable loyalty to the supreme leader is the watchword. The security network is not there for the well-being and protection of the citizens and their property; it is for the survival of the leader and the system.

Security is empowered to nip in the bud any dissent. Enjoying unchecked powers criminalisation of suspects and opponents requires no proof for necessary sanctions such as barbaric torture, elimination, kidnapping, prolonged incommunicado detention, disappearances, among others, as deemed fit. This system instils great pain in the ordinary citizens who have nowhere else to hide. While the citizens live in constant psychological torture, physical pain and reign of fear through systematic and persistent intimidation, harassment, torture, maiming, and elimination, the regime proclaims the absence of open protests, insurrection by the populace as evidence of social peace, contentment, loyalty and stability, whereas, in reality, the people have been caged.

To get unflinching loyalty of the personnel of the SEDOC and BMM, they were treated with lavished favours and free cash at their disposal. This special core constituted the political police whose mission was to fight suspects, dissents, subversion, and insurrection against President Ahmadou Ahidjo. They had no uniform and secrecy was the watch word. None pried into the affairs of the other to the point that two colleagues seemingly working together or on mission, each indeed could be spying on the other only to individually report to the boss. They enjoyed special privileges and monthly financial bonuses above their counterparts in other security departments. This was quite apart from Presidential treats that came periodically for those who did their work exceptionally well. Those who failed to merit such special awards were either transferred or denied the bonuses. It was thus a question of keen competition to excel in sadism to be recognised and recommended by he who had the President's listening ear for promotion, advancement, special Presidential envelope, among others. Here promotion or appointment was not based on measurable or verifiable meritocracy but on loyalty to the leader determined secretly by being efficacious in defending the interest of the leader. As the SEDOC and BMM were French-outposts for special tasks, without doubt, for many years after the so-called federal union, there were no Southern Cameroonians serving in these special security units attached to the Presidency. But many Southern Cameroonians were victims of this repressive outfit.

Some of these sadists were posted to institutions of higher learning at home and abroad where they posed as students, for example, but with an evil mission of spying and reporting periodically. Such also work in embassies.

In a totalitarian state as Southern Cameroonians have come to understand, the language of human freedom, equality, dignity and social justice disappears while overwhelming emphasis every second of the hour is laid on peace and order. The media and all other instruments of communication are used to instil fear in the masses in the name of guaranteeing public security, peace and order which the regime claims is necessary for 'development'. To instil fear and incapacitate the people the media is not free; it is grabbed, monopolised and gagged.

The evil dawn came with introduction of '*laissez passer*', the equivalent of the apartheid South African 'Pass'. Thus the Southern Cameroonian, who hitherto moved freely in his country like a bird flies in the air, was forced to report at the administrative office for a *laissez passer* to enable him move to other towns for whatever purpose. This was strange and intolerable. Next to be imposed was the national identity card, and the multitude of gendarme and police check points. At check points no one could rightly guess which documents would be demanded; *laissez passer*, national identity card, tax tickets, voter's card, as from 1966, the era of the CNU one party state, among others. If a traveller had all he could be asked to produce his vaccination card simply to make him pay a bribe to be set "free." Enforcement of *laissez passer*, national identity card gives wide room for terrible abuses, arbitrariness and corruption. The joy of independence was shattered within the split of a second and left all Southern Cameroonians gasping for speech like a fish removed out of water and placed on a rock in the Sahara desert. All this was in the name of ensuring public order, peace and security for the leader's survival.

But is this what they bargained for? Is this what the UN meant by "independence by joining?" Under this system, have British Southern Cameroonians achieved independence to enable them enjoy complete freedom and shape their destiny in conformity with UN Charter, the Trusteeship Agreement and UN Resolutions and their legitimate aspirations?

But what is public security without individual liberty? How can there be peace in society without human equality, freedom and justice for all? Is it the security and the wellbeing and happiness of the people that the state exits to defend and promote or it is that of the individual ruler? What is development without the opportunity for self-fulfilment of the citizen? How can a society be developed when the people caged live in constant fear of the unknown? What is development without human liberty?

Under the new order, Southern Cameroonians have learnt, painfully though, that the ruler is not the incarnation of the will of the people to whom he is responsible and accountable; he is for self and foreign interests. It is in this light that the role of the ruler has to be understood. Here the interest of the people and the state symbolised by the ruler and institutions were diametrically opposed. But the people are powerless for security apparatuses are exclusively answerable to the ruler and the individual actors cannot be brought to face justice for any heinous crimes they commit in the name of defending the leader and the system.

9

The Root of the Reign of Evil

French Cameroun under the policy of *"independance avec la France"* gave birth to or metamorphosed into la République du Cameroun and in form and character; la République du Cameroun inherited everything le *Camerounais Français*. *Independance avec la France* on 1ˢᵗ January 1960 did not give birth to a new nation with a new personality, core values upholding and enhancing the legitimate aspirations of the citizens with a distinct spirit, mission agenda and world view. No! While the black Camerounais replaced le Français at the helm of affairs in Yaoundé, the heartbeat of the state was/is monitored in Paris: it is simply to perpetuate French interest. It was destined to be an outpost protecting and promoting French interest in central Africa. Consequently, it was Southern Cameroons that had to conform under the crushing weight of annexation and the policy of assimilation under the veneer of national integration, a euphemism for annexation, uniformity, conformity, and colonial occupation to build the so called one and indivisible bilingual French Cameroun. But this was an unknown agenda to the UN and the British Southern Cameroons leaders of the day. This ignorance of the hidden agenda however does not exculpate them of acts of failing to respect the UN Charter and resolutions declaring independence the inherent and unquestionable right of each colony and trust territory.

To attain this lofty objective and decapitate the masses, it became necessary that the security apparatuses enjoy overwhelming powers and are placed above the law.

Consequently, the judiciary was pocketed and it functions as an arm of the executive power. By legalising torture, the judiciary functions to protect political repression. With this, heinous crimes committed under the guise of state security are shielded from public scrutiny and perpetrators are never tried in a court of law. In Cameroun national security is under the control of an uncompromising loyalist of the supreme leader. Like in Hitler's Germany where his loyal friend Heinriet Himmler was in charge of the notorious Schutzstaffel (or SS), under Ahidjo and Paul Biya the likes of Abdoulaye Mouyakan, who was trained directly by the French on the inhuman methods of torture, and Jean Fochive who perpetrated the most barbaric torture systems from terrorism days, readily come to mind. To this day and remembering the dark hot days of the state of emergency of 1992, a mere mention of the name Jean Fochive generates automatic cold sweats in many a Bamenda man in particular and a Southern Cameroonian in general.

Under totalitarian regimes, criminals preside over the fate of the innocent and patriots of the land. Genuine patriotism, which in point of fact goes contrary to the interest of the evil establishment, is diabolised and criminalised to perpetrate the rule of the dictator as "divinely ordained" and sustain the evil system that prolongs human suffering and degradation. Cohorts and agents present the rule of the dictator as divinely ordained and without him the state will sink into the abyss of calamities and disintegration. The ruler and the state are two sides of the same coin, indeed inseparable. He alone is ordained to incarnate the state and the state is never seen or imagined without him. And this is the make-belief forced down the throat of the gullible to sustain the system, effect self-perpetuation and self-succession. This is attained by imposing a Presidential Monarchy.

By pricing public order above individual liberties, justice, officials of the security apparatuses are immune from public scrutiny and reproach. This builds in members of this state institution a callous mentality of hate, distrust, hostility, holier than thou mind set, arrogance, nonchalance, against the ordinary citizens. The holy cows and the ordinary citizens do not belong to one another nor do they share common aspirations and nationalistic sentiments about the state. In a police state where there is no justice, for the judiciary is rendered impotent, the men in uniform are the holier than thou, and project an air of superiority and supremacy. Justice is for the rich and powerful members of the clan. Justice is sold and bought and corruption is endemic. Kleptocracy and greed fashion the true character of the state and indiscipline and repression sustain the barbaric system. The orphans, widows, the vulnerable of society suffer as they must while the powerful swim in legendary wealth as they want as the Church and intellectuals of society that should raise a strong voice against gross injustice condone and become collaborators of the evil system.

A police state is the hallmark of a dictatorial regime. Under this inbuilt system the relationship between the ruler and the ruled is held not by mutual trust and confidence but by mistrust and instruments of coercion for the purpose of exploitation and marginalisation of the down trodden and wretched of the earth. The relationship is like that of a cat and the mouse in the same house. Though in one house, they belong apart. Peace and order prescribed by the barrel of the gun for the sole interest of the ruler never translates into trust and confidence building. Rule which is not predicated on the consent of the ruled is arbitrary, illegitimate, illegal and can only endure for a season. But if those in position of influence succumb to seeking the crumbs instead of using their privileged positions to speak out against injustice, repression and exploitation of the marginalised of the society, the more the society will sink into moral and spiritual bankruptcy and even physical decay.

Dictatorship equally uses programmed elections to perpetrate the rule of one man. Mere elections and physical existence of a multitude of political parties do not make a system democratic for the ballot box could be used to mask tyranny. Having fashioned all state institutions to serve personal interest, it is very easy for an avalanche of several political parties to compete in an election just to sustain one man rule.

In Cameroon though the state imposed one party system has given way to mushroom political parties, the hitherto one party that has been in power since the granting of flag independence, controls all the state machinery thus making it impossible for the new opposition parties to defeat it at any election. The Union Camerounais, (UC) which has twice metamorphosed taking up new garments, namely, Cameroon National Union (CNU) in 1966, and Cameroon People's Democratic Movement (CPDM) in 1985, but inherently with the same heart, soul and mind, has ruled France's oversea territory of le Camerounais Français since independence on January 1, 1960. What the one state party has done in its interest by permitting the legalisation of mushroom political parties is; it has introduced '*Dictocracy*' and not Democracy.

Democracy is built on the will of the people to decide as to who rules them and how he who rules comes to the helm. Democracy is not predicated on the good will of an individual or a ruling party transforming itself by its willingness to permit other political voices to be heard. Inherent in democracy is inbuilt checks and balances, constitutional separation and devolution of powers, respect and defence of human rights and dignity, and the rule of law. Sovereignty rests in the people and not with the ruler. In a democracy the constitution permits the building of strong institutions and not strong leader with overwhelming powers. There is popular participation in decision making and the leader remains accountable to the people. There can be no democracy without a democratic culture and core values which shape the institutions that govern the state. The ruler governs according to the constitution which reflects the sovereign will of the people and he is never above the law.

In a post dictatorial state the building of a democratic culture must start with the democratisation of the state institutions. The constitution which is the organic law must be the product of the people's will and reflect their legitimate aspirations. Realistically such a constitution after due process must be approved in a referendum and not by a parliament overwhelmingly dominated by the ruling party, indeed the one state party of yesterday in a deceitful new garment. But in Cameroun the constitution has been the exclusive product of the ruling oligarchy and approved by the parliament heavily dominated by the ruling party members. The so called debate on the constitution which was crafted by the President's appointees, approved by the CPDM ruling party and signed into law by the President who is the President of the CPDM party in spite of the fact that the SDF MPs staged a walk out during the debate in the plenary session makes the so-called debate meaningless. Such an act disenfranchises the people and serves the purpose for which it was meant, namely, self-perpetuation.

In Cameroun the constitution is referred to as the organic law in theory, not in practice for the dictator uses the constitution, which is crafted at his whims and caprices, to defend his ambition to rule and reign. To begin with the so-called 1961 federal constitution was the amended 1960 constitution of la République du Cameroun which was imposed on British Southern Cameroons. It was simply an annexation law Ahidjo, as a foreign ruler, promulgated on 1st September 1961 and imposed on the UN Trust territory of British Southern Cameroons one month to the termination of trusteeship.

Secondly, Ahidjo's 1972 constitution was crafted in absolute secrecy by his French experts and imposed on the people.

And thirdly, though the SDF and Southern Cameroonian delegation walked out of the 1991 Tripartite Constitutional talks, President Paul Biya cared less and still had his 1996 constitution with Presidential mandate changed from five to seven years ramped down the throats of Cameroonians. Still determined to cling to power, in 2008 backed by the army which brutally suppressed popular uprisings against constitutional amendments, he removed the two-term limit of Presidential mandate, thus making himself life Presidential Monarch.

In the 1990s for President Paul Biya to hijack the struggle for genuine democratic change, he used the army and corruption to reject the call for the National (Sovereign) Conference and his monolithic parliament passed the so-called Liberty Laws of 1990. Enjoying the backing of the army, the security apparatuses and the judiciary of which he is the constitutional head, and using civil servants as his personal appointees, a consequence of his coercive machinery, President Paul Biya with the wave of his hand dismissed the popularly acclaimed National Conference with "La *conference nationale est sans objet*," and received a resounding applauds from his hand-picked CPDM parliamentarians. With the Liberty Laws Cameroon thus seemingly moved from one party to multi-party regime. But this has just been the creation of a window of opportunity for opportunists to use so called political party platforms to seek political space within the CPDM – hemmed political dictatorship. The CPDM having confiscated political power and with total monopoly over economic resources, military and judicial institutions has arrogated to itself supremacy and to any who recognises and accepts the status quo, a portion is given. This gave birth to the "Presidential Majority," a gang of hungry political rogues who cling on the coat tail of the ruling party to enjoy Presidential patronage from the national cake which the CPDM has confiscated and controls as if a personal heritage for self- survival and glorification.

Nothing explains this more than what happened during the 1992 Presidential elections, an election in which multiple political parties contested thanks to the indefatigable stance of the SDF overwhelmingly supported by Southern Cameroonians in whom democratic culture is still alive. *Le Camerounais Français* who never inherited a democratic culture and by the instrument of brutal repression were never allowed to build an indigenous one, a sad consequence of foreign influences, have never known and practiced multi-party democracy.

To buttress and substantiate the above argument the following dramatic acts are telling:

1. When Mr Andre Tsoungui, the Minister of Territorial Administration (MINAT) as boss of the elections hinted Mr

Paul Biya in 1992 that from returns pouring into MINAT the tables were not in his favour, the answer was quick in coming "...*je ne veux rien entendre. Je veux gagner les elections.*" (I do not want to hear anything else. I must win the election.) Paris in metropolitan colonial style decreed "An English man cannot rule a French Province." And the figures were doctored to perpetuate the system in the spirit of the Presidential Monarch, Mr Paul Biya.

2. To test the will of the system further, Ni John Fru Ndi, the supposed winner of the presidential elections, challenged the results at the Supreme Court, as allowed by law. The President of the Supreme Court, Mr Alexis Depanda Mouelle, acknowledged that there were irregularities but declared that his hands were "tied" and upheld the results as declared by the Counting Commission supervised directly by MINAT boss.

Though all international observers unreservedly recorded that the elections were heavily flawed and as such could not be accepted as meeting international standards of democratic elections, with the support of Paris, the army and the Supreme Court, the victor became the vanquished.

The point of going to the Supreme Court was futile exercise not just because Mr Mouelle, as his appointee was answerable to President Paul Biya but more so for the fact that President Paul Biya was/is the Chief Magistrate and Presiding Officer of the Higher Judicial Council. This makes the judiciary merely an extension of the executive arm of government. This further explains President Biya's conclusion that "*l'impossible n'est pas Camerounais*".

As if this was not enough, North West, the home Province of Ni John Fru Ndi, was placed under a state of emergency with Fru Ndi under house arrest and his lieutenants either incarcerated, for example, Justice Nyo Wakai, (rtd), my humble self, Nfor Ngala Nfor, or on the run for dear life, such as Bar. Lukes Sendze, John Mancho, among others. It was hell on earth in Bamenda and the North West Province, in general, within the three months of the brutal state of emergency. Either incarcerated or out of incarceration you were not safe so long as you were identified as an "*opposant*" and the Southern Cameroonian was simply, "*l' enemie dans la maisons.*"(the enemy in the house) as declared in 1990 by Mbombo Njoya, the MINAT Boss when the SDF was launched in Bamenda under military siege and blood bath.

Within this state of emergency human life and human dignity lost meaning. Torture, degrading punishment and maltreatment of those arrested and held under life threatening circumstances at the BMM and gendarme cells could only be likened to what took place in the days of terrorism in la *Camerounais Français*. And those armed with licence to freely use the gun having been fed with the notion of being in enemy territory were determined to nip the threat to the survival of their supreme leader and the state in the bud by making the people bend, conform, or crack. They came with fascist mentality and saw the Bamenda man as an enemy of the state. With vicious ambition and determination to make the Bamenda man submit; torture, grenades, the gun, were all at their disposal. Proconsul Bel Luc Rene, nicknamed, Grenade, reintroduced the long forgotten laissez passer. Kale-kales into different parts of the town and other towns and villages in the province were consistently systematic. Peeping through the window the message was simple; there were more soldiers in Bamenda town than civilian population. For his "good work" Bel Luc Rene was soon after deservedly rewarded with post of minister.

What we must understand here is that once a people are armed with hate language and believes and fortified with power of life and death over others for their own survival and glory, those hated are diabolised and criminalised. They become subjects of exclusion and even elimination. The real pain is felt through practical application and not through deceitful-sweet talk. They become sub humans in the eyes of their oppressors.

This reminds me of the incidence in Buea Gendarmerie cell in July 2000 when the francophone Company Commander after scolding us as if we were hardened criminals, asked one of his lieutenants to read Matthew 22:21 which states, "Render therefore unto Caesar the things that are Caesar's and unto God the things that are God's."

Satisfied with the reading he held a gun in his hand and with vicious arrogance told us that from the bible verse just read, he was at liberty to even kill us and would not be committing any crime. The question is, was he here equating Biya with Caesar or with God? Sadists make those they oppress to look up to their leader as super human being if not a demi god to be praised all times and worshipped.

As one so humiliated and with his right to life in a captor's hands, his calling for a verse to be read from the bible kindled some hope in me. I thought from within me if he knows God, believes in Him to the point of quoting from the bible, he would certainly be lenient to us.

I came out dam wrong and disappointed. The devil can as well quote the scriptures to back up his diabolic machinations. Thus the terror imbued Company Commander, whose name I had no means of getting that fateful night, descended harder on us after the reading. To him we were equal to diseased cows to be disposed of. We were at his mercy.

Lord Acton was indeed right when he declared; 'Power corrupts and absolute power corrupts absolutely.' Yaoundé has given unbridled powers to every proconsul, gendarme, police, and soldier, posted to Southern Cameroons. What started in 1961 has persisted to this day.

Here is the confessed spirit shattering experience of a college teacher in the carnage that took place in Ndu on June 6, 1992 dubbed, Black Saturday. The carnage was simply to annihilate the yearning for change through democratic process and perpetuate the CPDM rule thus the reign of the Presidential Monarchy. He mournfully recounts his ordeal:

"On the night of Tuesday June 9th '92 Ndu was under military siege. The Quarter where I live, Njipluh, seemed to have been a prime target. We arose that morning to be confronted by heavily armed gendarmes. I was arrested at gun point at my door… At about thirty metres from the main road we were ordered to get down on our knees and crawl the rest of the way. As we moved painfully along, the gendarmes beat and kicked us, belts, boots, truncheons, gun butts landed with force on our bare backs. I was so badly beaten that I sustained multiple bruises all over my body, including my knees and feet. After a lot of effort and endurance we arrived at the main road. We were still on our knees, and there we beheld a pathetic sight…men, women and children lamenting loudly. There we were forced to undress and were left naked wearing only our underpants. Shirts, trousers, socks, shoes, blouses, wrappers, money, documents (tax (tickets) and I.D. cards) were fed to a ready fire and burned before our eyes. The beating that followed was unbearable. The wailing that ensued was so soul shattering given the vicious beatings accompanied with kicks and blows. A blow of a belt on my left ear almost slashed it from my head…The bruises on my feet and knees, the weals(sic) on my back, the injury to my left ear, all indicated the torture and humiliation I had suffered. I stood naked and ashamed in front of my own children, bleeding and covered in mud."

Samuel Tanyi in broken spirit and will mournfully concludes, "Even as I write two women are incarcerated in the dungeons of Nkambe gendarmerie for no apparent crimes…innocent. Until the gov't changes its oppressive tactics and convince the people of its good intentions social and equal opportunity etc. the battle will rage on if only in our minds." (Ndi, Michael Ndi, 1995:39-40). But the famous U.S. President, Abraham Lincoln admonishes us, "To sin by silence when they should protest makes cowards of men."

To place a tight lid on the institutionalised system a multifaceted spy network, censorship and torture centres such as the BMM were made state policy. With the bush war led by the UPC that started against the repressive French rule in 1955 persisting, the Western and Littoral regions that border Southern Cameroons were permanently under a state of emergency. With so-called unification of 1st October 1961, four out of the six administrative divisions of Southern Cameroons came under the existing state of emergency. And on the heels of this came the spy network, censorship, the BMMs constructed in Bamenda and Kumba. These outfits which grossly undermine human freedom were strange and unbearable to Southern Cameroonians.

Thus Southern Cameroons instead of emerging into "independence" with joy she emerged into annexation and colonial occupation in tears, a broken spirit as liberal democracy and Westminster Parliamentary system adapted to Southern Cameroons socio-cultural milieu was promptly on that day 1st October 1961 replaced by a foreign imperial rule and the barrel of the gun whose agents, to imprint their distinct identity, spoke a foreign language, French. From this day Southern Cameroonians were disenfranchised as their inherent right to shape their destiny by being ruled by leaders elected according to their free democratic choice under laws fashioned by them in line with their core values and legitimate aspirations were confiscated and rudely replaced by foreign laws, a foreign system and imposed foreign leaders.

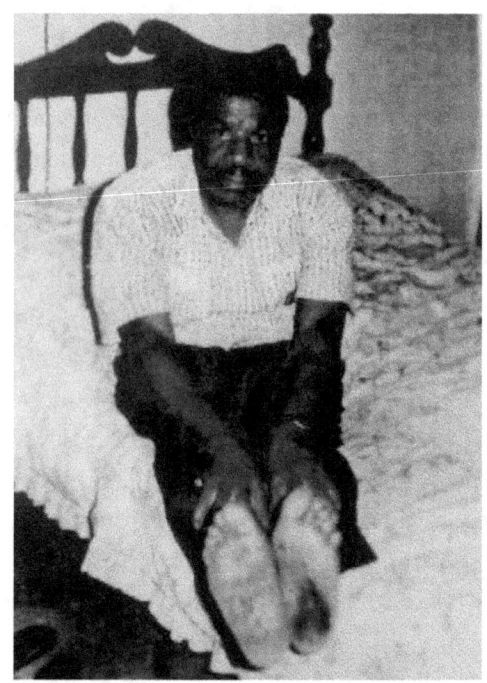

Joe Atakwana, victim of reign of terror

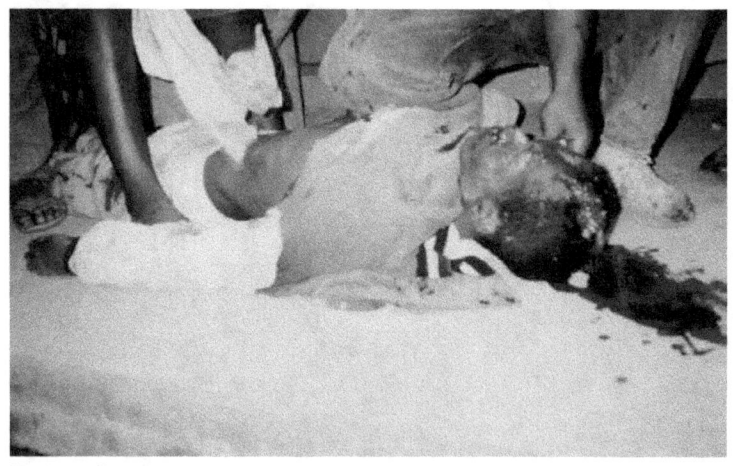

Reign of terror to perpetuate annexation

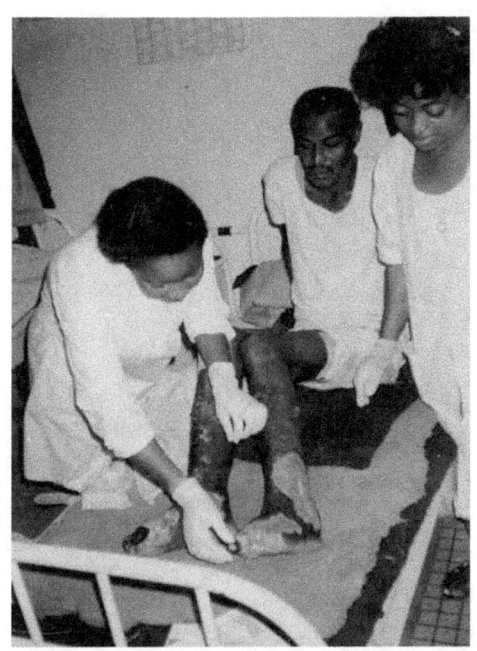

Pa Z. Khan, victim of brutal torture, died with these wounds after more than 11 years of imprisonment

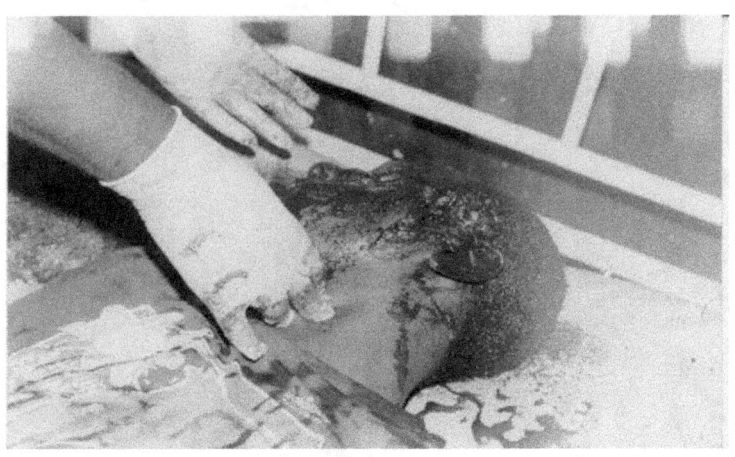

Ndenge Elvis, victim of reign of terror to perpetuate colonial occupation

10

It Knows No Limits

Within the established complex security network there are specialised units far removed from the ordinary man. These specialised units handle much of the dirty work. Men fit for such units are a special breed, quite often than not, recruited from particular tribes or ethnic groups notorious for barbarity and wickedness. The staffs of this complex security network are well shielded from public glare. In their specialised torture centres their victims cease to be human beings, they alone are "human" or even semi gods and their leader worthy of the worship of the sub human. They make you believe that, and sing praises to the leader for their entertainment. The better you do this submissively the higher your chances of being spared from persistent and systematic torture.

Victims are made to hang by the wrists or ankles from the ceiling before they are beaten. There is also the *balançoire* where one is tied both hands and feet on suspended pools like a goat for the roasting. From this suspended position you are made to swing- a kind of seesaw operated by electric power- while the torturer lands solid strokes on you. From the point the feet and hands are tied blood circulation is made ineffective. Many find their death, as happened during the Bamenda state of emergency, through this bestial torture.

The *balançoire*, a French invented torture system against the Algerian war of independence is such a barbaric tool of the devil all humanity should hate and condemn. It was by this system that Che Ngwa Gandhi found his premature death. This barbaric torture system sniffed out life from him on November 18, 1992. This is what the famous Pastoral Letter of the Archdiocese of Bamenda in mournful comments said of the death which made some wonder if Satan could have done anything worse. This is what the Pastoral Letter had to say:

> "The tragic death of CHE NGWA GANDHI, a death which came about as a direct consequence of the horrendous and utterly sadistic torture inflicted upon him, is an eloquent proof, if any proof were still needed, of the reality of torture which is daily inflicted, with impunity, upon our fellow Cameroonians here in Bamenda..."(p. 5).

Laid in state for burial on November 22, 1992 a cold solid sheet of darkness settled on Bamenda at noon day as wailing across the broad social strata was unprecedented. Why? He was no known militant of the SDF. A quiet gentleman working with a private establishment, he did his work according to the established roles. Circumstances of his arrest had nothing to do with the SDF or the presidential election result. Did some big gun seize the chaotic situation offered by the state of emergency to settle some scores?

Under a dictatorial regime torture, brutality, defies human understanding and logic. State sponsored terrorism against defenceless citizens, men, women and children is like action of an occupation force in a foreign land or an army against pirates on the high seas. It is simply bewildering how a state institution, maintained at public expense, which should defend the citizens, could so callously and viciously turn against the citizens, their wellbeing and dignity, in a make-up story of maintaining state security or public order when in reality it is for the maintenance of the status quo.

And because the media is not free, every act remains isolated and shielded while family members and close friends lick their wounds in quiet for fear of further reprisals. For the regime to remain clean before Western democracies, firstly it presents every opposition as agents of communism or terrorists. Secondly, foreign journalists and human rights activists are not allowed easy access into the country. With this Cameroon generally has remained a close society and underdeveloped with dilapidated infrastructure and terrible security checks by corrupt officials. This in general has killed even the development of the human potential and abundant natural resources that can attract foreign investors.

Determined to subject Southern Cameroonians to the rule of intolerance and slavish submissiveness, state sponsored terrorism in the name of "kale-kale" into Southern Cameroons towns, villages, plantation camps, sometimes in the dead of the night or early hours of the morning were rampant. To give you a true character of what this kale-kale which could decapitate a proud law abiding and peace loving people may I quote a child's eye witness account, a traumatising experience which he will live with unto his grave. This is the frightening account:

> "One rainy Saturday night, long past midnight, our camp was besieged by fierce looking soldiers of the Cameroon army. At the time they spoke what was perceived to be a foreign language (French). Doors were kicked open and truncheons used to rouse hard working, taxpaying and law abiding citizens from their beds. Our houses were looted; mothers, sisters and aunts were

raped. The men were herded unto trucks from Bota camp and dumped at the Victoria Community field where they were compelled to lie (sic) face-down in the mud.

"At dawn, wives and children went in search of their husbands and fathers. They were only released at midday when the sun was at its peak. The men looked like ghosts. My father had only a pair of shorts on with no shirt and no shoes. To add insult to injury a fresh wound was visible on the right side of his head. At the sight of my father, I held fast to my mother and cried. I was afraid to get close to him because he looked awful. On the way I tried to ask questions but was hushed down by the adults. At home I was brushed off with an unsatisfactory mantra: Kale-Kale! Kale-Kale!! I still remember feeling very hurt. ...I would later learn it was Mr Ahidjo's favourite method of quashing dissent. The population had to (be) cowed into total submission." (Chi Simon: 2009 pp.9-10).

These kale-kales like the "Laissez Passer", the equivalent of the apartheid South African "Pass," were all dictatorial outfits that grossly violate human rights and freedoms which Southern Cameroonians found to be unacceptable and intolerable. But with the army of occupation and spy network, they were spine-broken and powerless. The gendarme is ubiquitous and omnipotent. With the spy network came the ugly word "subversion" which covered a wide range of offences as determined by the authority concerned. The divisional officers, the direct representatives of the President, were/are above the law and have powers to detain any suspect for fifteen days renewable. In detention, such victims are subjected to torture, sometimes denied food, even the food brought by relatives. The sick are sometimes denied medical care even under sponsorship of family members. I suffered same in the Mamfe gendarmerie cell in September 2002. Detainees have died out of neglect, lack of medical care just the same as due to barbaric physical and psychological torture.

What we endured in the narrow world of the Bamenda Central Prison was a true reflection of how far Southern Cameroons had come to lose its identity, personality and moral authority. It reflected how far it had become an occupied territory, an appendage of la République du Cameroun. It reflected how endemic the culture of torture and the barrel of the gun rather than rule of law and faith of the people have tenuously held together the distinct two Cameroons. And all these reflect the evident inevitable consequence of breaking apart for self-survival for no people in perpetuity surrender to foreign domination and alien rule. Torture and repression as instruments of state policy can only last for a season and never forever for no matter how deep the cup of endurance may be, it must over flow when the right moment comes. Even green bananas in the depths of a deep freezer will get ripe when due.

Torture is evil. It is alien to the universally cherished concept of human rights and equality, human freedom and dignity. It is an abuse to the basic tenet of just punishment which must be commensurate with the crime after due process of the law based on a prescribed penalty for an established offence. It is a calculated assault on human dignity and grossly violates the natural law. Torture is illegal under international law. Any government that subscribes to democracy and the rule of law must proscribe torture at all cost.

Article 5 of the Universal Declaration of Human Rights (UDHR) adopted in 1948, declares:

> "No one shall be subjected to torture or to cruel, inhuman or degrading treatment or punishment." Here torture, for whatever reason finds no justification. It is completely forbidden thus to administer or create condition for so that loyalists violate international law.

Art. 7 of the International Covenant on Civil and Political Rights (ICCPR) adopted in 1966 states:

> "No one shall be subjected to torture or to cruel, inhuman or degrading treatment or punishment. In particular, no one shall be subjected without his free consent to medical or scientific experimentation." This treaty of UN Member states which came into force in 1976 after acceded to by the required number of states prohibits torture. This makes it binding on UN Member states that have ratified the treaty.

In addition to these the UN in 1975 made a land mark declaration on the protection of all persons against all forms of torture and degrading treatment or punishment. In Art. 3, it states:

> "No State may permit or tolerate torture or other cruel, inhuman or degrading treatment or punishment. Exceptional circumstances such as a state of war or threat of war, internal political instability or any other public emergency may not be invoked as a justification of torture or other cruel, inhuman or degrading treatment or

punishment."

What is most interesting about this UN Declaration against torture is that it was adopted by acclamation by the then 144 member states of the UN. Significantly this makes the prohibition against torture universal.

The African Charter on Human and Peoples' Rights (ACHPR) adopted in 1981 in its Art. 5 explicitly states:

> "All forms of exploitation and degradation of man, particularly...torture, cruel, inhuman or degrading punishment and treatment shall be prohibited."

Disturbed by the persistent application of torture by states and security agents in spite of the foregoing instruments, the UN has gone ahead to adopt 'Code of Conduct for Law Enforcement Officials,' (1979). In Art. 5, it states:

> "No law enforcement official may inflict, instigate or tolerate any act of torture or other cruel, inhuman or degrading treatment or punishment, nor may any law enforcement official invoke superior orders or exceptional circumstances such as a state of war or threat of war, a threat to national security, internal political instability or any other public emergency as a justification of torture or other cruel, inhuman or degrading treatment or punishment."

It is however sad to note that in spite of all these provisions forbidding torture, cruel and inhuman punishment or degrading treatment of human beings, in Cameroon and in dictatorial states in general, there is scant regards paid to these universal norms and the respect for human equality and dignity. Suspects are still tortured to extract information, confession, or to force opponents renounce their beliefs, denounce comrades while others are tortured to death. Kidnappings and disappearances are still rampant. Large sums of scarce resources are still wasted on building spy networks and torture centres by dictators determined to cling to power against the legitimate aspirations of the citizens. Dissent is not tolerated as *dictocracy* is imposed to perpetrate self-succession by hock or crock in place of democracy which upholds the sovereign will of the people.

Over the years, targeted repression of the 'Anglofools', i.e. the Southern Cameroonians, who are seen as outsiders and who must be made to conform, has inevitably helped to reinforce the 'Anglophoneness' or the Southern Cameroonian consciousness! The almost half a century co-habitation instead of bridging, has instead widened the gap of colonial inherited differences making separation inevitable for healthy staying apart. The co-habitation instead of building the much trumpeted, national integration, national unity and consciousness, it has built unity apart or exclusive solidarity for survival. This is but a natural responds to external hostility due to inbuilt hatred, discrimination, assimilation and naked exploitation of Southern Cameroons for the wellbeing of the self-proclaimed la République du Cameroun Monarch.

The fault is not that of the Southern Cameroonian, the treacherous foundation notwithstanding. The fault is that of the francophone who determined to monopolise and confiscate all state powers; political, economic, judiciary, and military has seen his success in reducing Southern Cameroons, a distinct nation within international law, into two provinces of its territory and the over five million Southern Cameroonians into objects of assimilation, repression and exclusion from decision making and power as self-beneficial.

The government has established an unwritten law which has barred even the most talented and loyal Southern Cameroonian from ever occupying certain strategic positions in the country such as ministerial departments of Finance, Defence, Foreign Affairs, Territorial Administration, Education, Public Service, Economy and Territorial Development, not to talk less of National Security, Secretary General at the Presidency, and the Presidency itself. This goes same with strategic public corporations such as the petroleum sector though the black gold is from Southern Cameroons soil.

This policy of exclusion of a people from position of influence and decision making became so self-evident after the Presidential Decree abolishing the Southern Cameroons Government in Buea in 1972. This, no doubt, is part of the structural policy of repression: the annexed do not enjoy equal rights and do not equally belong. This has had a dangerous spill over effect as all sectors of human endeavour see a Southern Cameroonian fit only for second fiddle.

In Yaoundé and Douala Southern Cameroonians have had to constitute development associations to build what has come to be known as Anglophone schools for the education of their children at the primary level while for post primary education many of the children are repatriated to schools in Southern Cameroons. Envious of the high quality education, thanks to inherited spirit of discipline and devotion of the teachers and the fact that the English language and the Anglo-Saxon culture dominate, the francophone, behaving in colonial master style, have come to flood their children in the schools thus reaping from where they did not sow. This, in future, is to deprive Southern Cameroonians even of the crumbs that fall from the master's table.

This discrimination and anti-Anglophone culture has not stopped there. The church has not been anything accommodating nor has it cried against this injustice and domination. Within the Catholic Church there exist Anglophone Parishes in Yaoundé and Douala; the existing churches could no longer accommodate the Anglofools, their contribution notwithstanding. While in la République du Cameroun territory you have Anglophone primary schools, colleges, churches, and cultural centres, among others, built and maintained by Southern Cameroonians, as they strive to survive within a hostile intolerant anti-social domineering environment, you do not have similar structures comparable in Southern Cameroons established by the francophone. The Presbyterian and Baptist denominations have had to do same by establishing churches to meet the needs of their flock. With the establishment of so-called bilingual schools in Southern Cameroons, everything is honey and butter for the francophone who in Southern Cameroons is lord of the manor.

The daily attitude of the francophone gendarme, police, and soldier, administrator who behaves like a colonial master in a conquered territory and does not in the least hide his disdain for the Southern Cameroonian, this in all respects reinforces the francophone consciousness against the Anglophone survival consciousness.

In addition to the daily treatment, either in Southern Cameroons or in la République du Cameroun, memories of Tombel, the two states of emergency, the economic blockade, code named *'Operation Daurade'*, May 26, 1990 Launching of the SDF, in Bamenda, Black Saturday June 6, 1992 in Ndu, SCNC Commemoration of Southern Cameroons Independence Day, 1st October 2001 in Kumbo and Bamenda, Buea University, 2005 and 2006 crisis, among others, reinforce the stark differences between the two peoples and nations of Southern Cameroons, and la République du Cameroun held together by a thin thread of brute force and illegal laws. This has inevitably pushed to the fore distrust and hostility on an unprecedented scale. Similar incidences on la République du Cameroun soil, for example, the state university crises of 2005, and the launching of political parties, never subjected the people of la République du Cameroun to any brutality, repression and extra judicial killings. Why only in Southern Cameroons?

The usual physical and psychological maltreatment the Southern Cameroonian suffers in the hands of his oppressor is never determined by the seriousness of the infraction but by this deep seated hatred and distrust the francophone gendarme or police has for the Southern Cameroonian-as enacted by the characteristic culture of colonial occupation. At the slightest excuse this generates the sadistic character in him against the hapless dis-empowered Southern Cameroonian. An Ndu victim's encounter says it all. I quote:

"I was arrested at 6pm from my house on that 6th June 1992 by six gendarmes. They ordered me to remove my shoes which I did. They took these and used in beating my jaws with to an extent that blood came out of my mouth.

"Before we arrived the Petrol Station, Ndu, they kicked my abdomen and smashed my stomach with their boots, tore my blouse and breast wear...

"Later came one gendarme call (sic) Albert, he accused me that I naked his wife- a police woman who works in Nkambe. This particular gendarme took two fat yellow pepe (sic).ground them with his hands and forced them into my vagina. It was unbearable. This was when I cried for help for hours in vain... After these tortures, I started menstruating without a pant or raper (sic). From the 6th June to the 10th I remain (sic) in cell without food or water..." After these four days "I was given my dresses that was when I managed to control my menses. In this brigade I was never allowed to see the sun, food brought to me by relatives and sympathisers was either poured or sent back." (Ndi, 1995: pp.50-51) Mary Bienna Kimbi, alias Iron Lady, narrated her experiences of hell on earth.

Later transferred to Nkambe and detained for long under life-threatening circumstances, persistent torture and without medical care, she finally succumbed into the cold hands of death due to barbaric torture she suffered in the hands of her captors and incurable complications that ensued there from. What a society in which pregnant women are arrested and subjected to sadistic torture and some in their nude before nude men are made to use their menses as body lotion! Even the devil will lament on his throne in hell for the Southern Cameroonian under la République du Cameroun reign of terror.

Most painfully, it should be pointed out that this carnage in Ndu went to extreme because of the local CPDM cohorts and collaborators whose greed to be in the good books of the Yaoundé master decided to betray their own people and settle scores. Worst reprisals come from betrayal when the few elect in society, in defence of self-interest instead of defending the vulnerable, treacherously turn their backs on them and collaborate with the invaders or oppressors. But we must understand that evil is contagious and has a boomerang effect. God avenges for the orphan, the widow and the weak.

Unknown to the Southern Cameroonian this sadistic character is a carry-over of the cruel crude abuses of the colonial era sanctioned under the *'indigenat'* in French Cameroun which conferred judicial powers on colonial administrators for a range of limitless offences. This was perfected by Ahidjo in concert with his French mentors to maintain power by brutally fighting a bush war against the UPCists. Absolute power cushioned by the confiscation of the judiciary and control of the national cake to corrupt those with weak spines in effect know no limits. In all these the Southern Cameroonian had no hand but has come to be a victim. He is a victim of arbitrary powers to cripple his spiritual will powers, decapitate his humanity and keep him perpetually subjugated. But for how long! Where on earth have a people been subjugated forever?

SCNC Nsongwa Village Women Exco, Bamenda

Commonwealth SG's Special Envoy after audience with SCNC Leaders is interviewed by Journalists, Bamenda.

Peaceful demonstration during visit of Commonwealth SG's Special Envoy, Bamenda

Nfor, & Mbinglo addressing the SCNC Youth Freedom Dance Group, after Rally, Mbort, Donga Mantung County

SCNC Rally, Mbort, Donga Mantung County

Nfor N. Nfor with SCNC USA, Peaceful Protest at UN New York, Memorandum submitted to UNSG, October 1 2004

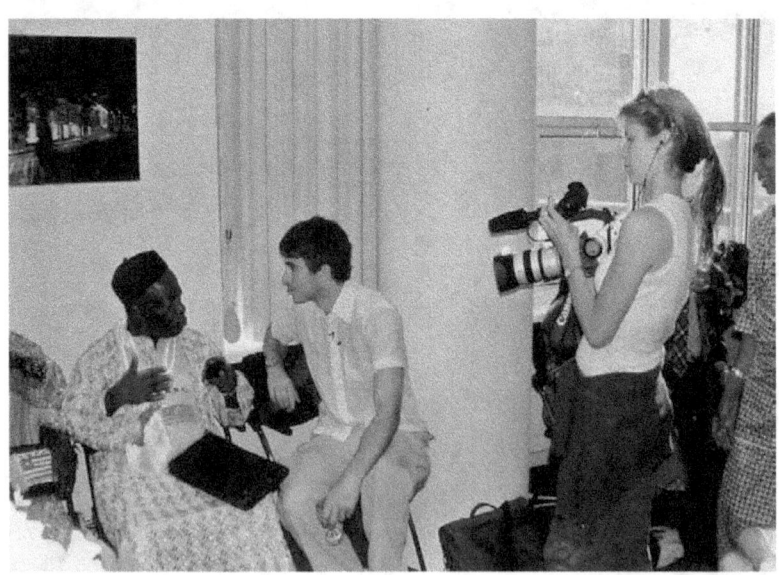

BBC Journalists interview Nfor N. Nfor for a documentary on emerging nations, The Hague

UNPO *led Peaceful Demonstration in Solidarity with SCNC and International Appeal for* FREE NFOR NGALA NFOR, *la Rep. du Cameroun Embassy, The Hague, 2005*

11

Fifty-Six Theses Justifying the restoration of the Statehood of British Southern Cameroons

A. Why were the SCNC Leaders arbitrarily arrested and detained? We were arbitrarily arrested and detained for speaking the truth about **The British Southern Cameroons Nation.**

B. What is that TRUTH? Is the Southern Cameroons a historical reality under international politics and law? Incontrovertibly, it is established that:

1. Before World War I, Germany had many colonies (protectorates) in Africa, one of which was German Kamerun. Kamerun became a German Protectorate following the Berlin Conference of 1884-1885. Before this date there had never been a kingdom or empire in Africa known as Kamerun or Cameroon.

2. Upon the defeat of German troops in German Kamerun by the combined forces of the United Kingdom, France and Belgium under General Charles Dubelle (British) in 1916, they affected a provisional partition of German Kamerun, giving birth to two distinct territories under international law, namely, British Cameroons, and French Cameroun. Following this provisional partition each colonial power set up separate administration, according to its colonial philosophy, within its sphere of influence for purpose of exclusive control and economic benefits.

3. The two separate Mandated Territories were created from the former German Kamerun which at the Versailles

Peace Treaty in 1922 ceased to exist as a fact of international law and that parts of German Kamerun today make up the francophone nations of Tchad Republic, Central African Republic, Congo (Brazzaville) Republic, and Gabon Republic. The other is part of the Federal Republic of Nigeria. Respecting international boundaries as defined by treaties and colonial heritage, la République du Cameroun is the successor state of French Cameroun and not the German Protectorate of Kamerun which, with the Treaty of Versailles, ceased being.

4. By the Milner-Simon Agreement which was ratified by the Versailles Peace Treaty of 1919 the international boundaries of British Cameroons and French Cameroun were sealed. By this act, comparable only to the Berlin Conference of 1884/85 that partitioned Africa into European colonies that partitioned Africa, the British Cameroons and French Cameroun became two separate entities of international law and politics. The Mandate Agreement and Trusteeship Agreement which Britain and France, respectively signed with the League of Nations in 1922 and in 1945 with the UN, were treaties emphasising the distinctiveness of the territories with their defined boundaries and maps of the respective territories attached.

5. As separate entities of international law and politics the two Cameroons became mandated territories of the League of Nations formed after World War I.

6. On assuming responsibility for the political future of the two territories, the League of Nations placed one part of the Cameroons under the United Kingdom Administration, while the other sector came under French Administration, thus the designations British (Southern) Cameroons and French Cameroun, respectively.

7. From March 1916 the United Kingdom and France, after the collapse of the Condominium, each, as of necessity, put into effect in their respective territories, administrative, political, legal, economic and cultural systems that was totally exclusive. This gave birth to the contradictory personalities, philosophies of life, and worldview that distinguish the Southern Cameroonian from the *Camerounais Français*.

8. The United Nations Organisation (UNO) which succeeded the League of Nations after World War II, created the Trusteeship Council to supervise the Trust territories (the former Mandated Territories) to Self-Government and Independence in conformity with Art. 76(b) of the UN Charter. Most remarkable and worthy of note is the fact that from the League of Nations to the United Nations Organisation, debates on the political future of any these territories, subjects of international system, there was never reference to Germany as a consequence of WW1 and the Versailles Peace Treaty.

9. Under the Trusteeship System both the Cameroons under United Kingdom Administration and Cameroun under French Administration were equal in status and were registered under Category "B" Trust territories.

10. Recognising its obligation to the World Body and moral responsibility to the people of the British Cameroons, Her Majesty's Government signed the Trusteeship Agreement committing herself to respecting the *"Sacred trust"* and ensuring the progressive development of the people of the Trust Territory towards Self-Government and Independence.

11. For forty-five years, the Anglo-Saxon liberal democratic culture, scientific and methodical approach to issues, a deep sense of the common weal, which inculcates the spirit of tolerance, honesty, sensitivity, integrity,

transparency and accountability, was made a way of life and the foundation of national culture in the Southern Cameroonian.

12. The French colonial policy of assimilation as rigorously applied in French Cameroun split the colonised society into *"les citoyens"* and *"les sujets"*. This combined with paternalism imbued in the *Camerounais Français* a dependency complex which ties him to the apron strings of Paris making him believe in the superiority of anything French (remember the French civilising mission which made every educated elite and business elite regard France as "home"). The *Camerounais Français* is individualistic, aggressive, and intolerant and has no sense of the common weal. He has a grabbing culture, is corrupt and embezzlement is his hallmark. The urge to enrich oneself at the expense of the state, the citizens eulogise it as *"à la Camerounais"*, and their President defends it as *"Cameroun c'est le Cameroun"*, and *"l'impossible n'est pas Camerounais"*.

13. Consequent upon this, Southern Cameroonians are referred to as "Anglo fools" because, comparatively, they don't use given opportunities to serve self-interest. They are tolerant, sensitive, hardworking, more caring, obedient, and honest and treat public property as belonging to the state and should be used for the good of all. But persistent repression is destroying the humane qualities in those assimilated who believe in the theory that while in Rome do as the Romans.

14. A nation bankrupt of a national culture based on core values that hold society together or a society whose ethical values have been replaced by self-interest is crime-endemic. Consequently, it nurtures sycophants and leaders who behave like mercenaries to their nation. Le *Camerounais Français* and a Southern Cameroonian are as un-mixable as water and palm oil. They are like darkness and light, which due to inherent

natural forces though part of a day, will forever be apart.

15. The Southern Cameroons and la République du Cameroun, though constituting part of the African Continent; their distinctive historical, cultural and ideological backgrounds are direct opposites which any effort at fusing is bound to bring calamity. What God had put asunder (in 1916) let no man try to put together by force of arms and decrees.

16. The U N General Assembly Resolution 224 (III) of November 1948 protected Trust Territories from being annexed by other states. The Trust territory of the Southern Cameroons, as a distinct political entity in international law is thus forever protected from annexation by any neighbouring country, including la République du Cameroun, formerly, the UN Trust territory of Cameroun under French Administration.

17. Respecting this UN Resolution neither the United Kingdom, as the Administering Authority, nor Nigeria with which the Southern Cameroons, for purpose of convenience was administered for nearly half a century, made any effort to assimilate and annex the Southern Cameroons.

18. As precondition for attainment of Self-Government and Independence, the UN Trusteeship Council in discharging its duty in conformity with Art 76 of the UN Charter, sent Visiting Missions (4 in all) to the Southern Cameroons to assess the political and socio-economic development of the territory. This equally applied to French Cameroun and each report was considered on its own merit with the respective Administering Authorities answering questions for clarification.

19. In 1953 seeing that the interest of the Southern Cameroons was not well protected, Southern Cameroons Members of Parliament in the Eastern House, Enugu, and in

the Federal House, Lagos, as well as Cabinet Members, declared "Benevolent Neutrality" in Nigerian Politics. To this effect they gave up all their rights and privileges to fight in defence of the legal identity and self-government of the Trust territory of the British Southern Cameroons as provided for by the UN Charter and other international instruments.

20. This patriotic spirit of the Southern Cameroons political leaders yielded great dividend. At the Mamfe Conference in 1953, Southern Cameroonians, respecting their international status, unanimously resolved to petition Her Majesty's Government for the creation of a separate Southern Cameroons Region with its own government and legislature.

21. In 1954, cognizant of the special status of Southern Cameroons under International law and respecting her right to self-determination, a new Constitution came into force which made the territory a separate region with its own Government and House of Assembly in Buea. Brigadier E.J. Gibbons, C.B.E. was appointed Commissioner and as H.M's representative was the President of the House and the Executive Council.

22. The Southern Cameroons House of Assembly met for the first time on October 26th 1954, and by a subsequent Motion sponsored by Hon John T. Ndze of Nkambe Division, October 26 became Southern Cameroons' National Day, replacing the Empire Day, May 25.

23. The Southern Cameroons attained Self-government in 1954 with Dr E M L Endeley as Premier, while French Cameroun attained Self-government in 1957, three years later, with Mr Andre Mbida as Premier. Each functioned separately building its international personality as guided by its

Administering Authority and the international system.

24. In 1959, Mamfe, the cradle of Southern Cameroons nationalism, was once again host to a political jamboree to decide the political future of the Southern Cameroons.

25. From the evidence before us the purpose of the 1959 Mamfe Conference (called at the instance of the Administering Authority and code named, the "Plebiscite Conference"), was to undermine Southern Cameroons nationalism and right to self-determination in order to violate Art. 76(b) of the UN Charter and the Trusteeship Agreement.

26. Disturbed by the diabolic tactic of withholding the right to self-determination of Southern Cameroonians, Fon Achirimbi of Bafut, speaking for the Traditional Rulers described Nigeria as "Water" and French Cameroun as "Fire". He concluded, *"Sir I support secession without unification."* He, reflecting majority opinion, favoured Southern Cameroons achieving full independence as of right in conformity with the UN Charter and legitimate aspirations of the people. The conference ended without a consensus.

27. By UN General Assembly Resolution 1352 (XIV) of 16 October 1959 the Southern Cameroons was separated from Nigeria in preparation for the latter's independence in October 1960.

28. This separation was in conformity with the special status of the Southern Cameroons as a UN Trust Territory. At separation, the internationally defined and recognised boundaries were respected consonant to the Anglo-German boundary treaty of 1913 and Anglo-French boundary Treaty of 1931 and other international instruments in force.

29. On the strength of this UN Resolution the UN Trust Territory of the Southern Cameroons was not part of

Nigeria when it (Nigeria) attained independence on October 1ˢᵗ 1960 as the Federal Republic of Nigeria.

30. On October 1ˢᵗ 1960 the Southern Cameroons new (Constitution) Order in Council 1960 S.I. 1960 No 1654 came into force and by this constitutional development the Southern Cameroons was enhancing its national institutions for sovereign independence.

31. The UN sponsored and controlled plebiscite of February 11, 1961 was an imposition through colonial intrigues and manipulation, which led the World Body to violate its own Charter. From evidence before us it was not the place of the UN to insist on organising a plebiscite in a trust territory enjoying full self-government. Southern Cameroons was entitled to sovereign independence in conformity with the UN Charter and UNGA Resolution 1514 of 1960 and if found beneficial go into a federal union with another sovereign nation on mutually agreed terms. "Independence by joining" could never have been in the best interest of the people as it was in contradiction of UNGA Resolution 1514 and the UN Charter.

32. In the UN Plebiscite of February 11, 1961 Southern Cameroonians voted to form *a Federation of two States of EQUAL STATUS* with la République du Cameroun, the successor state of French Cameroun as contained in UN DOCUMENT "THE TWO ALTERNATIVES" which served as the Manifesto for the plebiscite. The Plebiscite was not in itself an instrument of union; it was a mere declaration of an intent subject to comprehensive negotiation and mutually agreed terms voted overwhelmingly for secession and to form a Federation of two States of EQUAL STATUS with la République du Cameroun. The UN DOCUMENT "THE TWO ALTERNATIVES" which served as the

Manifesto for the plebiscite was very explicit on the nature of the federation. It was to be a loose federation with a bicameral parliament, the central government left with limited subjects and more subjects under the jurisdiction of the states. The plebiscite in itself was not an instrument of union; it was a mere declaration of an intent subject to comprehensive negotiation and mutually agreed terms.

33. By law, only Southern Cameroonians were eligible to vote in the UN sponsored Plebiscite. By barring *le Camerounais Français* living and working in British Southern Cameroons from voting, this in itself points to the fact that the two Cameroons nurtured under different colonial powers, like the two Congos, and the three Guineas in Africa were/are distinct entities under international law; similarity in name having nothing to do with their respective rights to self-determination and independence.

34. On January 1, 1960 French Cameroun achieved independence and became la République du Cameroun. It was by this name, la République du Cameroun, that the new independent nation joined UN membership on September 20th 1960.

35. On April 19, 1961 the powerful (political) 4th Committee of the UN General Assembly, by 50 "YES" votes, 2 "NO" votes, and 12 Abstentions, *overwhelmingly voted for the Independence of Southern Cameroons. By the same act October 1st 1961 was declared the Independence Day of Southern Cameroons. La République du Cameroun, France and other French speaking African countries, except Mali, failing to block the vote walked out of the Hall.*

36. By Resolution 1608 (XV) of April 21, 1961 the UN prescribed a post plebiscite Conference at which modalities for the formation of the UN-envisioned FEDERAL UNITED CAMEROON REPUBLIC between the Southern

Cameroons and la République du Cameroun were to be worked out. These modalities include the adoption of a federal constitution and an ACT of UNION which should have been signed by J. N. Foncha, for the Southern Cameroons, and Ahmadou Ahidjo, for la République du Cameroun. Participants at this crucial conference as designated by the UNGA were the Government of the Southern Cameroons, the Government of la République du Cameroun, and the Government of the United Kingdom as the Administering Authority. This conference being part and parcel of the UN controlled and supervised plebiscite, indeed the agenda-package for transition to termination of trusteeship and granting of independence, should have been convened and presided over by the UN. Had this conference taken place and an Act of Union adopted, a copy of the mutual agreement should have been deposited with and published by the UN General Secretariat, in conformity with Art. 102 of the UN Charter.

37. UNGA Resolution 1608 (XV), that was key to this UN-envisioned federal union was never implemented because la République du Cameroun, France and all French-speaking African countries except Mali voted against the UN-envisioned federal union. No legal union, according to UN prescription was thus formed. The plebiscite itself was not an instrument of union. It was only a promise Southern Cameroonians made to the UN and not even to la République du Cameroun.

38. The co-habitation of the Southern Cameroons and la République du Cameroun that came into effect on October 1 1961, known as the Federal Republic of Cameroon, was between two equal sovereign independent states. To this effect none was to surrender its identity, independence,

territory, natural resources, and population to the other. Each came into the non-treaty loose federation strictly preserving its territorial integrity, governmental system – political system, judiciary, administrative system, educational system, socio-cultural values and language as inherited from its Administering Authority. The federation between the two nations was not a territorial union; it was a loose non-treaty inter-governmental association at the top, namely, federal level. It was a free association of two independent states. Every human product has its expiration date buried within.

39. Cognizant of this reality Art.47 (I) of the Federal Constitution stated that "Any proposal for the revision of the present constitution which *impairs the unity and integrity of the Federation shall be inadmissible".*

40. This was an entrenched clause of the constitution and any violation of this constitutional provision was bound to herald the demise of the co-habitation or loose federation, with the obvious consequence, namely, restoration of exclusive inherent identities. But this, notwithstanding, the union concocted consequent upon colonial manipulation was maintained by fraud and killed by intrigues, anti-constitutional manoeuvres and force of arms of la République du Cameroun, the partner that had a hidden agenda.

41. The 1964 OAU Summit in Cairo, Egypt, declared colonial boundaries inherited at independence inviolable. This OAU Resolution and Art. 4(b) of the AU Constitutive Act all emphasis the immutability and inviolability of boundaries inherited at independence. This action by the African continental body conforms to the international principle of *uti possedetis juris* and the *critical date*. By endorsing this OAU Resolution President Ahidjo very well knew the colonial boundaries between la République du Cameroun and the

Southern Cameroons inherited on January 1, 1960 and October 1, 1961 their respective dates of independence.

It should however, be recalled that the two Cameroons did not attain independence at the same time under a common name to make it one and indivisible but as two distinct nations. In the preservation of their respective inherent characteristics and exclusive core values and as it is conventional with all associations between nations each retained its inherent personality and right to withdraw from the loose federal union if not satisfied with the treatment it receives from the other partner.

42. The United Nations grants independence to a dependent territory only once. Independence once granted is never revoked.

43. In May 1972 President Ahidjo as a dictator carried out a coup against the loose federation in which he used military force to dissolve the co-habitation or loose federation and imposed a Unitary Government with him as the President and Head of State. The post of Vice President as was under the loose federation was abolished. Abolishing the federated state governments and dissolving the federal assembly he ruled for one year by presidential decrees.

44. President Ahidjo carried out this coup at a time when coups were fashionable in Africa. Only in a coup can the entire constitution or large parts thereof be suspended and the governmental structure changed as radically as happened in 1972 with one man ruling by decree.

45. The demise of the federation implied the end of the loose association made up of two independent nations. But that la République du Cameroun, after having destroyed the loose association, has, like an expansionist power, occupied the territory of the Southern Cameroons, now reduced to

two provinces of la République du Cameroun, is great cause for concern as it threatens peace and stability in the sub region.

46. Because the Southern Cameroons has been annexed by la République du Cameroun, the territory is occupied by francophone administrative and military personnel and its rich natural resources are exploited, for the exclusive development of la République du Cameroun. Southern Cameroonians are denied their political, economic and cultural rights. Subjected to foreign domination and alien rule, they are a stateless people on their own land.

47. Annexation, which results in the domination of a people by another, is contrary to international law and conventions, which defend democratic principles, human dignity and the equality of all nations big and small. The African Charter on Human and Peoples Rights in Article 19 states;

"All Peoples shall be equal; they shall enjoy the same respect and shall have the same rights. **Nothing shall justify the domination of a people by another."**

48. Though the Southern Cameroons accounts for 70% of the GDP (thanks to petroleum), Southern Cameroons never receives more than 4% of the investment budget. Ndian County, in Southern Cameroons, which produces the black gold, does not even have a petrol station, an inch of tarred road and petrol is far more expensive in Southern Cameroons than in la République du Cameroun.

49. Though SONARA (French acronym for the Petroleum Company) is located in Victoria the top management staff is francophone, while more than 90 per cent of the other staff are still francophone. The official language is French. The company, of course pays, royalty to

the Douala City Council in la République du Cameroun instead of to Victoria City Council in Southern Cameroons.

50. President Ahidjo abolished the loose Federation and annexed the Southern Cameroons so that the oil money goes into the black account", in French, *"compte noir"* known only to the President, a francophone, his francophone Director General and mentors in Paris.

51. Southern Cameroonians are deliberately impoverished to keep them perpetually subservient, beggarly and subjugated so that they lose their self-dignity and some among them are used as toys to betray one another in order to receive favours from the francophone boss. But, regrettably, these traitors are not and can never be trusted by the francophone who believe in the natural order of things that a traitor remains a traitor. A traitor is extracted from his own kind and used and once the mission is attained, he is dumped.

52. After the dissolution of the federation and annexation of the Southern Cameroons all Southern Cameroons industries and economic infrastructures, such as the Electricity Corporation (Powercam), Santa Coffee Estate, the Produce Marketing Board, the Development Agency, Cameroon Bank, Victoria and Tiko seaports, Tiko International Airport, the inland air strips of Besong Abang, Bali and Weh, the Cameroon Air Transport, (CAT) etc., were deliberately closed. The purpose has been to cripple Southern Cameroons economically and perpetually making it look like an economic appendage of la République du Cameroun.

53. The restoration of the statehood and independence of the Southern Cameroons is an inalienable right of Southern Cameroonians recognised and defended by international law, the UN Charter, the African Union Charter,

the Universal Declaration of Human Rights and the African Charter on Human and Peoples' Rights. Under the principle of self-determination it is held that the supreme interest of every nation, large or small, rich or poor, is the right to self-existence.

54. The UN General Assembly during its 50th Anniversary Celebration in 1995, adopted the declaration contained in document A/AC240/1995CPR11Rev.1 reaffirming:

> *"the right to self-determination of all peoples, taking into account the particular situation of people under colonial or other forms of alien domination or foreign occupation and recognising the right of peoples to take legitimate action, in accordance with the Charter of the United Nations to realise their inalienable right of self-determination."*

55. In their legitimate quest to restore their self-identity and sovereign independence, Southern Cameroonians cannot be accused of 'secession'. Southern Cameroons and French Cameroun evolved as two distinct nations and attained independence within their respective defined territorial boundaries under different circumstances, on different dates and on their respective merits. Like in the demise of the Senegambia, for example, which enabled each of the two nations, namely, Senegal, and The Gambia, to restore their respective sovereign independence, in like manner, the dissolution of the loose association empowered each partner Southern Cameroons, on the one hand, and la République du Cameroun, on the other, to restore its separate independence and sovereign existence. You cannot secede from what you were never a part. The over flogged and trumpeted idea of one and indivisible Cameroun is a distortion of history and a

make-belief. It does not hold water. It is the figment of the imagination of the Yaoundé colonial regime and its lackeys.

56. The Southern Cameroons National Council, (SCNC) currently led by Dr Martin Ngeka LUMA, is not a political party. It is an irredentist movement, a nonviolent liberation movement, indeed, the collective will of Southern Cameroonians that embraces all shades of ideological and religious views, men, women and youths of all ethnic groups and social status for the singular mission of liberating the Southern Cameroons from the annexationist claws of la République du Cameroun. By fighting for the right to self-determination and the restoration of the statehood of Southern Cameroons within its inherited international boundaries so that Southern Cameroonians live in complete freedom, dignity and happiness, we are doing God's will. For this reason, we, your leaders, languished in prison. But by the mighty hand of God, we are winning. Southern Cameroons will be FREE.

C. But what prompted the arrest and detention of SCNC leaders on Oct. 1, 2001?

Southern Cameroons leaders and all the defenders of the restoration of the STATEHOOD OF THE BRITISH SOUTHERN CAMEROONS massively turned out on *1st OCTOBER 2001* to commemorate the 40th Independence Anniversary of their country, the *Southern Cameroons* though confiscated by expansionist la République du Cameroun.

To perpetrate the annexation and occupation of the SOUTHERN CAMEROONS, the Yaoundé regime let loose its occupation forces that had been reinforced, to attack, brutalize, kill and detain peace-loving and law-abiding citizens of Southern Cameroons, engaged in peaceful celebration of their independence as granted by the UN in 1961. The arrests, torture and detention were all over the country and in Kumbo for example, three people Boniface Laigha, Amidu Bel Suika, and Terence Sela were murdered in cold blood while many were wounded by the repressive forces that opened fire on unarmed jubilant celebrants. A fourth person died later in hospital.

It is however instructive to take cognizance of the fact that in celebrating the 30th Anniversary of its independence on January 1 1990, under President Paul Biya, la République du Cameroun issued a commemorative postage stamp worth 1000 FRS CFA, which bears the map of French Cameroun as it attained independence on January 1 1960. Each dependent territory is granted independence within internationally defined and respected boundaries. The Biya regime by putting up the map of la République du Cameroun and strictly respecting the colonial boundaries inherited at independence was by this act demonstrating its commitment to the respect for the sanctity and inviolability of colonial boundaries inherited at independence as declared by OAU Summit in 1964, Art. 4(b) of the AU Constitutive Act, and by the principle of international jurisprudence known as *uti possedetis juris*. This principle totally rejects territorial expansionism, which is the handiwork of dictators and totalitarian regimes. By arresting, detaining, maiming and killing Southern Cameroonians, who are being treated as a conquered people, the Yaoundé regime does not want Southern Cameroonians to identify with their past, defend who they are, and be masters of their destiny.

As it is with a slave who is not even called by his real name, let alone allowed to neither talk of his ancestors, history, culture nor celebrate his birthday; Southern

Cameroonians suffer all imaginable indignities under the occupation forces - administrators, gendarmes, police and soldiers - of la République du Cameroun. Cognizant of the fact that nothing in their favour justifies their occupation of the Southern Cameroons, the Yaoundé regime depends solely on the brutal use of force to intimidate, terrorise, harass, oppress, rape and murder Southern Cameroonians so that they surrender to annexation and neo-apartheid the worst form of colonialism comparable only with apartheid of South Africa.

Yaoundé will be most comfortable if Southern Cameroonians can grumble in their beds and bleed to death. This is tolerable for no one outside will hear and ask, why? But to complain aloud and demonstrate, that is an unpardonable sin for someone outside this triangle of revolting illegality and relative peace will hear and ask a question. This is why whenever this sea of uneasy calm is showing signs of ripples CPDM cohorts are urged and encouraged with fat envelopes to pour in motions of support to drown the noise of waves.

The UN General Assembly on 14th December 1960 adopted Resolution 1514 (XV) by which it pledged to end all forms of colonialism.

The Resolution states:

> "*Recognising that the peoples of the world ardently desire the end of colonialism in all its forms;*
> "*Convinced that all peoples have an inalienable right to complete freedom, the exercise of their Sovereignty and the integrity of their national territory;*
> "Solemnly *proclaims the necessity of bringing to a speedy and*

unconditional end of colonialism in all its forms and manifestations.
"And *to this end*
"Declares *that*

1. "The subjection of peoples to alien subjugation, domination and exploitation constitutes a denial of fundamental human rights; is contrary to the Charter of the UN; is an impediment to the promotion of world peace and co-operation.

2. "All peoples have the right to self-determination, by virtue of that right, they freely determine their political status and freely pursue their economic, social and cultural development.

3. "Inadequacy of political, economic, social and educational preparedness should never serve as a pretext for delaying independence.

5. "<u>Immediate steps shall be taken in Trust Territories, Non-self-Governing territories or all other territories which have not yet attained independence, to transfer all powers to the peoples of those territories without any conditions or reservations in accordance with their freely expressed will and desire without any distinction as to race, creed or colour, in order to enable them to enjoy complete independence and freedom.</u>" (emphasis mine).

As no human community or race wilfully surrenders to annexation and servitude, nor submit to extinction, so are Southern Cameroonians resolved to regain their self-identity and complete freedom by restoring the sovereignty of the Southern Cameroons, their Fatherland. The Southern Cameroons is the only earth-space Southern Cameroonians have on this planet earth; the only heritage they have to bequeath to their descendants. To surrender is to deny their inalienable right as human beings and to existence in dignity. It will be the worst crime for this generation to deny their descendants a heritage and place of honour in history.

Like the former trust territories of Eritrea and Namibia, for example, that successfully restored their independence; our inherent and inalienable right to freedom is predicated on the restoration of the statehood of Southern Cameroons with its seat at the UN. A nation that provides conditions for self-fulfilment of its citizens, indeed a progressive nation, is one whose destiny is in the hands of its patriotic and visionary citizens and is ruled by consent of the governed.

Poems

Lament

February 11, 1961
When the axe of
Conspiratorial colonial intrigues
Tricked the UN to violate
The mission of its own birth to humanity

With "independence by joining" imposed
Cowardly, Southern Cameroonians
With their feet in concrete
And consciences chained
To two, and only two evils
They took a devastating faltering step.

From across the Atlantic
The land of the burning flame of liberty
Had cried Ambassador Zabloiski on UN floor,
Let the people have their independence
Unification promises political disaster

In native Mamfe Fon Achirimbi
In concert with the gods and ancestors
In prophetic language had said it all,
French Cameroun is "FIRE!"
We must be we and we only.

Oh Colonialism! Colonialism!
A creation of the evil mind
The bane of people afflicted
The reign of man's greatest evil
That dehumanises man
Making him lower than the ape

Oh Lament! Lament! Lament!
Hear the innocent souls
Weeping and sobbing in agony
Oh watch the cursed widow
Bemoan the gushing blood
Of her son bayonetted on her doorstep.

Oh watch the trigger-happy
Gendarme raiding and raping
Looting and vandalising
The land is cursed
Violence, terror is the constitution
Of the Southern Cameroons annexed.

Lament! Lament! Lament!
But in agony, extreme agony
The old in wisdom dream dreams
And the youths in aspirations see visions
Patriots are born, the masses reawakened,
And history of national rebirth
Is written in courage of patriots
And collective positive action
Rights the wrongs of yesteryear.

YES, THE NEW DAWN IS HERE!!

New Dawn Dream

I had a dream
Of Southern Cameroons reborn
Out of new nationalistic consciousness
And renewed communal spirit.
With blooming patriotism.

I had a dream
Not of a glorious past
But of a future
Great transformation
And prosperity.

I had a dream
Of Victoria berthing
In ocean going liners
And the wharves stocked full
With goods of all nations.

I had a dream
Of jubilant crowds and dancers
At Tiko international airport
Welcoming foreign dignitaries
For an African Union Summit.

I had a dream
Making a trip northwards
Towards Kupe and Kilum
To drink deep
Of this great transformation.

I had a dream
Driving from Victoria to K Town
It was on a supper high way
And in K Town I saw
A boisterous commercial centre reborn

I had a dream
Of the dead island Mamfe
Of mud and wanton neglect
Adorned with streets of marble
And the Cross-River emptying its trade goods.

I had a dream
Of new towns sprouting like mushrooms
And schools adorned with flowers
Along the Victoria - Bamenda high way
It was all commerce and life abundant.

I had a dream
From Mamfe to Widikum
From Widikum to Batibo
From Batibo to Bali then Bamenda
I was flying on land.

I had a dream
Sailing the Bamenda Ring Road
From Bamenda to Ndop then Kumbo
From Kumbo to Nkambe and Wum
On the renaissance supper Ring Road

Overwhelmed with joy and surprise.
I screamed

This can't be Southern Cameroons
And a soft assuring voice answered,
"It's the Southern Cameroons reborn"

Yes, I had a sweet dream.

We Have Come Of Age

We have come of age
Determined and resolved
To take no orders from
Any foreign authority
However powerful it may be.

For forty agonising long years
Have we been tossed about!
And kicked like pre-adolescents
Who know not?
And cannot defend their interests.

Like babies we were worth,
Being seen and never
To be heard and respected.
The most talented were fit
Only for sinecure posts and vice.

Like a conquered land
The occupation forces
In vandalistic style left in ruins.
Flourishing state institutions and towns.
Files, documents of our statehood

Were with glee put to the torch.

No! We have come of age
The fortunes of Southern Cameroons
Are, by Divine mercy and law ours
To make or mar
But to make for our good
Is our patriotic duty.

Under the SCNC banner
The Southern Cameroonian Youth
Soldiers for self-fulfilment
A bright new dawn where
With the Southern Cameroons restored.
The sky will be the limit.

Welcome Buea Reborn
Yes, we have come of Age!

13

Conclusion

"In Chains for My Country: Crusading for the British Southern Cameroons" sets out to present what SCNC leaders went through when they were arbitrarily arrested on 1st October 2001 and incarcerated at the Bamenda Central Prison. It is equally a testimony of the true state of affairs in the occupied land and the inferno every Southern Cameroonian is made to endure once he stands up for his inherent right. This only goes to confirm that every Southern Cameroonian is a prisoner of conscience, even the unborn in the mother's womb. This does not in the least exclude those who betray their kind to survive or in order to benefit from the crumbs that fall from the master's table.

Not here being the devil's advocate, could it not be said that some in this category are pushed by circumstances? Do some not only lack the spine to stand up erect? And being victims of an evil imposed condition succumb to overwhelming temptations? Could it not be said had they their way they would have preferred their rightful place of honour? Who, being man, will stand among his own and proudly declare that he survives on crumbs from his master's table? It could thus be concluded that the survival ethic is by nature an imposed condition which must be fought against to give man his rightful place as ordained by his creator.

The purpose is not to curry sympathy for the prisoners of conscience, it is to project to human kind, most especially to the UN and UK, what has befallen British Southern Cameroonians, who as victims of botched decolonisation process have had their rights of sovereign existence confiscated. Art. 76 (b) of the UN Charter and UNGA Resolution 1514 of 1960, which define the political, economic and cultural rights of Trust Territories and dependent territories are very clear. Here briefly stated, colonialism, foreign domination and alien rule have been declared a crime against human dignity, and human equality. And to enable man develop his full potentials and enjoy his complete freedom as endowed by his creator, the world body decreed that all Trust Territories and colonies should be granted independence. What needs be added here is that neither Art. 76 (b) of the UN Charter nor UNGA Resolution 1514 prescribe any preconditions for attainment of independence; an inherent and unquestionable right of victims of foreign domination and alien rule. Independence is a right due to all people under international law.

What must be stated without mincing words is that the UN was misled by some colonial powers determined to continue preserving their global interests to grossly violate its own Charter and Resolution on ending colonialism in all its forms and manifestations. British Southern Cameroons no doubt, is a victim of international colonial conspiracy against the sovereign will of the inhabitants. British Southern Cameroons, a shining example of democracy and the rule of law in colonial Africa, is in the third millennium a colony of la République du Cameroun. Through international colonial conspiracy, the UK, the Administering Authority of British Southern Cameroons, not respecting the "Sacred Trust" on midnight of 30th September walked away abandoning British Southern Cameroons to Ahidjo and la République du Cameroun army to annex and colonially occupy the territory. La République du Cameroun army backed by French imperial troops had been fighting a no nonsense bush war since 1955 against the UPC nationalists turned terrorists in the districts bordering British Southern Cameroons. In 1961, the army and the gendarmes came into British Southern Cameroons with the mindset of expanding the area of control to haunt down the enemy of the state. With this mindset, British Southern Cameroons was not a friendly territory to the defenders of the status quo and French interest, it was a potential hide out for the rebel forces out to destabilise a young independent state in the full embrace of French neo-colonial interest.

Consequently British Southern Cameroonians who went to bed on 30th September hoping and expecting a new sunrise on October 1st, 1961, their independence day, were most disappointed and traumatised when they saw but gendarmes armed to the teeth giving them matching orders in a strange language- French-to squat in the dust or mud depending on the region of the country the individual was caught.

Manifesting all anti-people behaviour and brute force, they never talk or speak to you; they scream and shout as if you were deaf and a mile away. The act of shouting and scolding is deliberate to cow you down and prove to you your impotence and helplessness. With their fingers always on the trigger this was/is a constant reminder that your life is in their hands and could be sniffed out at will without any apology to be given to anyone.

What British Southern Cameroonians of this age must know as a reality of human history is that God the Creator in his infinite wisdom did not create some people to be the carriers of water and wood for those who have by force of arms imposed their superiority over the subjugated. Foreign domination, alien rule and assimilation are evil condemned by the creator. Any system, individual that promotes or surrenders to is guilty before man and God. God created all men free and equal.

And throughout human history we have also come to know, as a reality, that it is always the subjugated that fight to set themselves free from bondage. The oppressor has never willingly set the oppressed free. Those who subject you exploit and decapitate you to make it impossible for you to challenge the myth of superiority and their imposed authority over you. They mislead and distort your history making their role appear the natural order of things.

The subjugated have never developed. Why? Because they are not masters of their own destiny. Once subjugated you lose your inherent right over your life, land, natural resources and your destiny. Foreign laws are imposed and the natural resources of your land are exploited for the benefit of your oppressor. The oppressed are forced to provide labour free of charge while the oppressor enjoys the sweat of your labour without any compensation. The subjugated and oppressed have their destiny confiscated for the benefit of the oppressor.

Destiny here means the future, your inherent right to a befitting future, a place of honour and dignity. Every parent and every age is duty bound to bequeath a rich legacy to descendants. To bequeath a rich legacy to descendants demands that you must be in control of your condition. You must equally be thinking positively of the future. A bright and worthy future is never a given, you work for it. And you work for it by proper planning. For a people to shape their destiny they must be united by bonds – a history, a culture, a territory, and a vision – that builds in them a consciousness of we as opposed to them. They must set boundaries, a dividing line, within which they are the masters and within which they must allow no intruders.

The greatest asset of man is not his physical built and energy. If it were left to this, man will never stand the elephant or lion and control other natural forces. Man's greatest gift from his Creator is his ability to reason. And for a people or a nation their greatness does not lie in the geographical size, the large population and abundance of the natural wealth buried below the surface of the earth and in the depths of the territorial waters. All these are nevertheless important. But a nation's true greatness lies in the wisdom of its people. This simply means the ability to think properly, use time and resources effectively which means in a manner to multiply production quantitatively and qualitatively and to guarantee similar conditions of production for future generation. This is critical for future generations have equal rights over the heritage as the current generation.

Wisdom is gained from experience and effort put into doing what is worth doing. Wisdom is acquired through exchange of ideas, experimentation, deep thoughts and reflections, effort to reach out, understand the nature of man, his origin and hereafter, human society and the world at large. It is by thinking positively to master our environment that we come to understand and it is by understanding that we believe.

Nations that are great are nations whose people are endowed with wisdom. Unless hard work is based on wisdom, the hard work could be counter-productive even to the individual who is exerting a lot of energy over and over many hours. Slaves under their masters and fearing the cane and other punitive acts work so hard but acquire no wisdom for they work against their will and never enjoy the fruits of their labour. They work not out of their own conviction and planning nor do they have control over what they do but work to please their master who imposes his plans and interest on them. Such instinctive works never make them develop for they are not in charge of their destiny. Living at the mercy of their masters, they do not even control their lives. They gain no satisfaction from what they produce and their descendants inherit nothing from their parents' sweat except servitude if their parents did not set themselves free.

England did not come to establish a vast empire over which the sun never set because she had the largest population with many hardworking giants. England is a small island nation but was blessed with patriots endowed with wisdom and sense of time management – never postponing what must be done today. English today is the number one language spoken across the entire globe – they spread it for they were determined to be the masters and shape the world for their collective good.

What great natural resources did England have to dominate the world? Was it gold, diamond or oil? The greatest resource of any nation is the people. But a nation that is annexed and occupied has her people in chains. And since the greatest asset of a nation is the people that project the nation making her proud among other nations, it is the subjugated people who must concert, unite and in courage rise against and defeat foreign domination and alien rule.

The people through their history and collective consciousness must organize and plan to overthrow foreign domination and alien rule to assume their deserved station among the free people and states of the world.

For the annexed, the colonially occupied to regain their collective self-consciousness of we as opposed to their enemies, they must resent their condition, hate and be determined to cut off the string that ties them to the enemy. They must be resolved to break the yoke of bondage. They must price what they have lost consequent upon foreign domination and alien rule above the imposed status of a subjugated people. A people who deeply and evidently become restless with their dehumanised status, who are discontented with the chains they go around with in the name of Prefectoral orders and multiple check points by aggressively-looking and trigger-happy and aggressive foreign forces on their roads, people who have identified the cause of their misery and mass poverty in the midst of plenty, who are discontented with their disenfranchised status in the sense that they no longer rule and direct their affairs, are people who becoming conscious of their destiny are determined to break with their ugly past and in triumph gallantly match into freedom. Here unity of purpose, a developed focused nationalistic consciousness married with time management are very essential for the desired deserved result.

Time management is concerned with making the best use of the circumstance for your own good. Firstly this begins with self-autopsy and identification of your position within the cosmos and total rejection of foreign imposition, an inward determination not to be missing in the crowd, not to be taken for granted, but to be recognised and counted among as an equal. It starts with standing up erect and not bending down for your enemy and oppressor to ride on your back.

Secondly, it deals with rejecting to be controlled, to be on your knees receiving orders and spoken to scornfully and dictated to by any person or human force. Right to the defence of self- existence, to be heard and respected by others is the only means to be reckoned with as an equal. You are never given equal rights but everyone will recognise and accept your equality and humanity once you project and defend your worth. You bow down to any dictates by man you will be made to remain bowed. For a people to willingly submit to a subordinate status and accept a subordinate role is to betray God's will for any people and bargain away cheaply their inherent right to dignity and the destiny of their descendants in dignity.

The more we think and reflect deeply on the condition or state of affairs and stop believing anything those growing fat on our misery and mass suffering; the quicker we will discover the door opening in front of us. There is always an alternative. Any human evil against a people lasts as long as the victims tolerate!

When the door you know or you were shown, is closed, don't give up and surrender to fate. When you surrender, you block the power of reasoning. But when you reject the imposed status as unworthy of your being and reflect on the history of other peoples who once were in your situation you will see an alternative door to the one closed.

You were not born to be a slave of la République du Cameroun or any other people. Once you give up resisting, once you surrender you make the enemy invincible. You were not made a toy in the hand of the gendarme or your oppressor. You are reckoned with only when you are master of your destiny. Being a master of your destiny is the surest means of guaranteeing and preserving the future. British Southern Cameroons must be restored as a distinct nation, free and equal to la République du Cameroun and other sovereign nations to guarantee the future of her descendants in dignity, equality and prosperity.

Through international colonial conspiracy in 1961, the door to sovereign independence through effective decolonisation was closed consequent upon the imposition of "independence by joining" and the non-implementation of UNGA Resolution 1608 of April 21, 1961.

The straight and defined open door which should have enabled British Southern Cameroons to emerge as a sovereign independent nation was decolonisation in conformity with Art. 76(b) of the UN Charter and UNGA Resolution 1514.

The hard choice facing British Southern Cameroonians of this age is either to judiciously exploit the opportunity offered by international instruments for any people subjugated under annexation, foreign domination and colonial occupation and free them- selves or to perish under alien rule. To the advantage of British Southern Cameroons are the peoples of Namibia, Eritrea, East Timor, Estonia, among others, who getting discontented with annexation and foreign domination and alien rule, did not surrender, they victoriously rose up against foreign rule and restored their respective nations to independence.

British Southern Cameroons has a very rich history which must not be allowed to rot away under the debris of la République du Cameroun's annexation and colonial occupation. Having attained self-government in 1954, three years before la République du Cameroun, and had a buoyant parliamentary democracy, two chamber legislature, effective separation of powers and deep respect for the rule of law, imbued with deep sense of human freedom, equality and dignity; we cannot turn round to surrender to the foreign rule of a dictator. By this we betray the shining will of God and compromise the future of our descendants. Before British

Southern Cameroonians of this age is just one choice to make, namely, the urgency to right the wrongs of 1961 by restoring their nation to national sovereign existence in order to bequeath a befitting legacy to the youths and unborn descendants. They merit no less. And we cannot afford to betray them.

Bibliography

Albert Mukong, *Prisoner Without A Crime*, Nubia Press, 1989.

Chi Simon Ndeh & Quifoor E. Mou-Chi, *Betrayal?* Patron Publishing House, Bamenda, 2009.

Ndi, Michael Ndi, *Naked Truth About That Ndu Genocide, (The Tongue of an Eye-Witness)* Riena Arts, Onitsha, Nigeria, 1995

Nyo Wakai, *Inside The Fence*, Patron Publishing House, Bamenda, Cameroon, 2000

Richard Joseph, (editor) *Gaullist Africa: Cameroon Under Ahmadou Ahidjo*, Fourth Dimension Publishing Co. Ltd, Enugu, 1978.

Tatah H. Mbuy, *Africa's New Experience In Multi-Party Democracy, (A Modern Challenge For The Local Church)*, Printed by Arnold Bright Printers, Owerri.

____*Pastoral Letter Of 29-11-1992*, Archdiocese of Bamenda, Charity Press, Mankon, Bamenda, Sunday, 29th November 1992.

____*Torture In The Eighties, An Amnesty International Report*, London, 1984.

____*The Holy Bible* (Men's Devotional Bible-New International Version)

www.ingramcontent.com/pod-product-compliance
Lightning Source LLC
Chambersburg PA
CBHW050538300426
44113CB00012B/2156